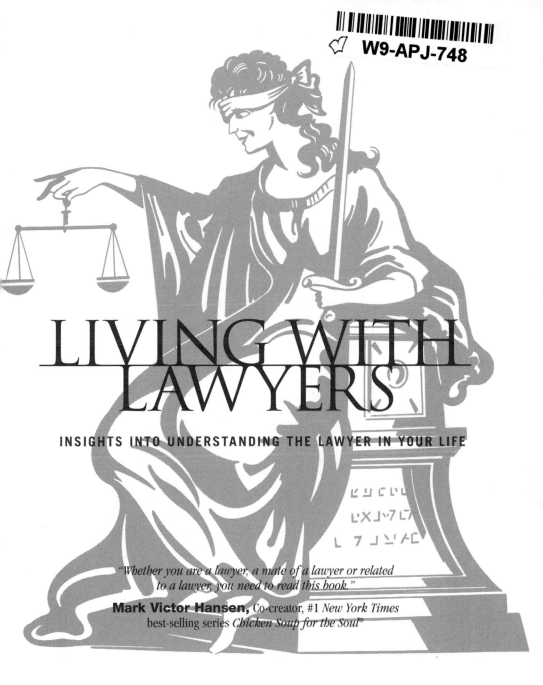

LIVING WITH LAWYERS

INSIGHTS INTO UNDERSTANDING THE LAWYER IN YOUR LIFE

"Whether you are a lawyer, a mate of a lawyer or related to a lawyer, you need to read this book."

Mark Victor Hansen, Co-creator, #1 *New York Times* best-selling series *Chicken Soup for the Soul®*

FIONA H. TRAVIS, PH.D.

FRANCES M. WEINER, M.A.   **JULIA R. DEVILLERS, M.A.**

Printed in the United States of America

01 02 0 9 8 7 6 5 4 3 2 1

ISBN: 09678906-2-4

Design: Heather Travis and Geer and Associates, Inc.
Copy Editor: Debra Pack

For more information contact:

Quarry Publishing

1-866-LIVELAW or
info@livingwithlawyers.com

"If you are living with one of America's nearly one million lawyers, this book is a must for you. Lawyers can be aggressive, direct and, at times, downright intimidating. *Living With Lawyers* provides keen insight into the lawyer personality and provides practical, useful advice about the challenges of living with such a personality. After reading this book, you will have learned healthy strategies, practical skills to make your relationship stronger, and you may even love your lawyer more!"

Steven C. Bahls, Dean and Professor, Capital University Law School

"A much needed book! Many marital therapists will rejoice once they read this book. It is a much needed book for working with people from a very high risk profession. BRAVO!"

John Gottman, Ph.D.
Author of *The Seven Principles For Making Marriage Work*
Professor of Psychology, University of Washington, Seattle

"Whether you live or work with a lawyer, *Living With Lawyers* will help you improve your relationship. And when you've finished, give this book to that lawyer in your life as it's also a good read for, and will provide insightful information to, him or her."

Hindi Greenberg, President of Lawyers in Transition and author of
The Lawyer's Career Change Handbook

"Attention lawyers: this book is for you. Not just for people in relationships with lawyers, *Living With Lawyers* is a book for lawyers to read to gain insight into themselves."

Angela Bosworth, Esq.
Director of Member and Professional Development Services
Ohio State Bar Association

"*Living With Lawyers* is an essential resource for anyone—spouse to secretary to coworker—who 'lives' with a lawyer. It offers practical insights and a compassionate approach to understanding the lawyer in your life."

Barbara Braham, business consultant and author of 12 books,
including *Be Your Own Coach: Your Pathway to Possibility*

"A 'must read' for those who work with or love (usually!) an attorney. *Living With Lawyers* is a great starting point for neutral, effective dialogue about what it means to have the Law in your life. A great gift for attorneys, law students, those who work with them, and their families!"

Lynn Steger, Assistant Director of Admissions, The Wellington School,
Columbus, Ohio and wife of a lawyer who practices International Law

"BULLSEYE—this book is right on target! Legal support staff who work with lawyers day in and day out will thoroughly enjoy this book."

Cathy Hankins, Certified PLS
NALS: The National Association of Legal Professionals

"I'm married to a lawyer. This fascinating book gave me the validation I need."

Jeff Herman, Founder, The Jeff Herman Literary Agency

This book is dedicated to:

Quinn Rachel DeVillers, Jack Hamilton DeVillers, and Nathan Craig Travis, who bring joy and love into our hearts every day and represent the hope for future generations.

and in memory of:

David Marmor, Findlay and Helen "Nellie" Henderson and Oswalt and Mildred Travis, whose love was responsible for motivating us to higher achievement, and whose spirit continues to support us through our difficult times.

Acknowledgments

To our husbands: Alan, Sam, and David

Living with you gave birth to this book. Your hard work, love and devotion to the law and our marriages has been a driving force in our lives. Thank you for your support, your strength and for believing in us. Without you in our lives, this book would never have been written.

To the spouses, families, significant others and those who work for attorneys:

Thank you for sharing your personal experiences with us and for urging us to write this book.

Table of Contents

Chapter 4

Loving Your Lawyer Without Losing Yourself..... 66

Chapter 5

Stress Happens: To Both You and Your Lawyer........................... 86

Chapter 6

From Our Point of View......................... 120

Preface

A Lawyer's Perspective

About 15 years ago, we contacted Dr. Fiona Travis to seek help with a number of issues. One of the major issues was the very real stresses on our relationship as a result of the demands put on lawyers. After intensive coaching during that time and, in recent years, occasional "tune ups," I offer a few thoughts about what can happen if you and the lawyer in your life work together with the ideas and concepts that Dr. Travis has set forth in this wonderful book, *Living With Lawyers.*

The law is indeed a demanding profession; some have called it a "jealous mistress." Without Dr. Travis's wisdom and insight into these demands on our life, I do not believe that my spouse and I would still be married and that I would now be enjoying—yes, enjoying—the practice of law.

At first, my spouse did not understand or appreciate what I did to earn a living. Indeed, she resented the huge investment of time and energy necessary to build a successful career. I also thought, early on, that the profession my spouse chose required a smaller investment. I finally learned that being a good lawyer did not require as much investment as I thought it did and my spouse finally learned that it required more than she originally assumed. This is an example of a key "truth" that you will learn when reading this book. And also, you will learn—how to listen, really listen, and then how to respect your different perspectives. You will learn together how to invest in your relationship—I'm talking about spending time focused on your spouse's needs and interests—so you can build a relationship of mutual respect.

In this book, you will also learn how to make meaningful "deposits" into your relationship, so that when you have to make "withdrawals," you can do it without breaking the "bank." For example, I learned that if you surprise your spouse every now and then with some extra time devoted to her, you'll be forgiven when, two weeks later, you have to break a promise to go out to dinner. Investing in the emotional savings account is well worth your while.

If you have children, they will benefit by you reading this book as well. I've told my children what a lawyer's world is like and they do care. I've told them what I have to deal with partly so that they can understand when I do not handle my stresses well and partly so that they can build a library of information to make wise career choices. I've also found that telling them what is going on, without revealing client confidences, causes them to be interested in my life. That makes me feel less alone in dealing with my stresses.

As a lawyer, many of our relationships with other lawyers involve fights—some cordial and some nasty. We must learn that we have to turn off the fighting side of our personality before we get home. Our spouses, children, parents, siblings and friends are not the enemy and we should not treat them like it. As my spouse has often said in so many words: "Treat me instead like your favorite client: Don't fight with me; keep your promises; and, every now and then, take me out to dinner or give me a nice present."

I've been a litigator for most of my 15 years in private practice. One fact I know to be true: If we are to be litigators, we will not control the courts, our fellow lawyers, or anyone else for that matter. So, we have to accept that fact. We can try to have colleagues working on cases with us who can cover for us, or even take over, when we get overwhelmed by the things we cannot control. If that is not possible, we need to accept the fact that we are not perfect and that we can only do our best. (Boy, that was hard for me to write! I'm still practicing that one!)

If after reading this book, your spouse only cares about how much money you bring home or about who is taking out the garbage, then perhaps you picked the wrong spouse. But, don't make that decision until you've completed not only reading this book, but also using the words as if Dr. Travis were personally "coaching" you in your relationship. Use *Living With Lawyers* as a guide so you practice becoming more sensitive to each other's needs.

So, what I am saying is this: Both my spouse and I know, from personal experience, that you can change your life. It is not too late and you are not too old—unless deep down inside you want it to be. You can have the time to laugh and play, the time to be curious, even spontaneous and sometimes irresponsible.

If you are the spouse, friend or maybe the legal secretary of a lawyer, take comfort in the fact that there is hope for your lawyer. Keep reading and put into action a little of what you learn each day. Be patient; growth takes time.

If you are a lawyer, when you feel as if your life is overwhelming, do not be afraid to make a call to someone like the author of this book, bare your soul and listen to the wisdom. I'm not suggesting that life will be perfect after you practice what this book teaches, but life with your lawyer (and as a lawyer) can be much better than it is now.

The Coached Lawyer

A Spouse's Perspective

When the "coached lawyer" speaks about spouses not understanding the investment necessary for a successful law career, I would like to add that lawyers, or lawyers-to-be, are so focused on their goals that they often lose sight of the sacrifices they expect from their spouses. Often these sacrifices are made without any communication with the spouse, just under the assumption that "this is what it takes." The mindset of "our whole relationship/life is about the law" is often the attitude that leaves a spouse feeling as if the relationship has little to do with the spouse at all.

When we first began talking with Dr. Travis 15 years ago, I feared our marriage would always be like a courtroom battle. Winning was the ultimate goal, and words were our weapons. I am very verbal myself, but I lacked the formal legal education to make me a professional "word-smith." Our approach to communication became less and less about hearing and understanding each other, and more and more about finding the perfect words to make the other understand our point. We wanted the victory of the verbal "touché!"

Without knowing it, I had entered the legal arena. Precise meanings became more important than feelings. It was not unusual for us to rush to a dictionary to find the "correct" definition. What we needed as humans, as partners, and as individuals got hopelessly lost in the fray.

It was only after coaching that I began to trust in my needs and feelings, and how I expressed those things so important to me. I quit battling over semantics. I learned to tell my spouse to "listen to what I'm feeling" and not to listen for "errors" in my words or thoughts so he could quickly be ready with a rebuttal. This, of course, was contrary to his training for the law. But, after many unsuccessful years of trying to change him, trying to talk like him (and not like me), I learned I was most successful at being heard if I could clue him in to how I wanted him to hear me. Often that verbal cue from me helped him change gears.

When we first married, I had every intention of being a very supportive spouse. What I wasn't prepared for was the law demanded much more than that. It demanded all of my spouse. He felt I didn't understand what it took to be a successful lawyer. I felt his goals and dreams not only superseded mine, but literally wiped them out. It was only after we learned to plan those dreams together, as well as include some of mine, that our lives together were really that—together.

The Coached Lawyer's Wife

About the Authors

Fiona Travis received her B.A. from Muskingum College and her master's and doctorate degrees from The Ohio State University. Her primary work is that of a psychologist whose private practice of 25 years emphasizes the unique stresses of the legal profession. Dr. Travis is a popular speaker to the legal community having presented to local and state bar associations, the Judicial College of The Ohio Supreme Court and to support staffs of law firms and the Ohio Prosecuting Attorneys Association. She is the author of several articles on the interaction of the body and the mind and presented her work to her colleagues of the American Psychological Association at conferences in the United States, Mexico and Canada. Dr. Travis is an Adjunct Professor on the Graduate Faculty of The Ohio State University and is a member of the medical staff of Mount Carmel Medical Center.

Dr. Travis has a lifetime of experience living with a lawyer. Her husband, Judge Alan Travis, is an Ohio Common Pleas Court judge. During 38 years of marriage, Dr. Travis has lived with a law student, private practitioner, Assistant Ohio Attorney General, Assistant Prosecuting Attorney who argued twice before the United States Supreme Court, and Bar Examiner for the State of Ohio. Currently, Judge Travis presides over the Common Pleas Court in Columbus, Ohio where he has repeatedly been selected the top-ranked judge on the court by attorneys of the Columbus Bar Association. Dr. Travis and her husband have two married sons and a grandson.

Frances M. Weiner is a summa cum laude graduate of Capital University and holds a master's degree in counseling from the University of Dayton. She is a Certified Community Mediator and Personal Life Coach. She has been living with a lawyer for more than 23 years. Her husband, Samuel B. Weiner, is a noted criminal defense attorney. Listed in "Best Lawyers of America," he has held numerous positions of leadership in the legal profession, including President of the Ohio Association of Criminal Defense Lawyers. Weiner is a career wife, dedicated to the quality of her personal relationship, and is sought as a personal coach by spouses of other attorneys. She has been a mentor to many by sharing her pearls of wisdom for achieving a happy and healthful relationship with a lawyer.

Julia DeVillers holds a master's degree in journalism and is the co-author of several books, including *You Can Make it Big Writing Books: A Top Agent Shows You How to Develop a Million-Dollar Bestseller* with Jeff Herman and Deborah Levine Herman (Prima, 1999) and two books slated for release in 2001. She has lived for nine years with husband and lawyer, David DeVillers, Assistant Prosecuting Attorney, voted the Outstanding Assistant Prosecutor by the Ohio Prosecuting Attorneys Association in 1999. David DeVillers is Director of the Gang Unit in Franklin County, Ohio, where his cases include prosecution of serial killers and gang slayings. As a result, she is currently guarded around the clock by police bodyguards. She has two young children, a daughter and a son.

INTRODUCTION

"The Law: It has honored us, may we honor it."
Daniel Webster

Living with a lawyer is a unique situation, with unique stresses and unique joys. It is a situation with which only other people in the same situation can relate. Yet, it is one that is not often addressed. Lawyers are bright, verbal, rational, articulate, competitive and excellent problem solvers. The personality traits many lawyers share, the stresses they face in their job, and the way they are perceived by society, all affect their relationships with other people. In fact, the very characteristics that make lawyers successful in the courtroom and in the field of law are the same characteristics that can create problems in their intimate and personal lives.

Living With Lawyers will help empower you in your relationship with your lawyer. Of course, when we refer to "your lawyer," we are not talking about the attorney who reviews your taxes once a year or the attorney you call when your neighbor tries to sue you again for your barking dog. We are referring to the lawyer with whom you have a relationship—marriage, dating, friendship. Or perhaps (s)he is your coworker or boss.

This book is not a recipe or boilerplate for successful living with your lawyer. Nor is it about getting your lawyer to change who (s)he is. It is not about suggesting lawyers need therapy, although we do refer to those who have changed through the healing, therapeutic process.

Rather, *Living With Lawyers* provides the wisdom gained from our clinical practice, research and professional experiences. It is designed to help you identify and make sense of "lawyering patterns" and how they can affect your relationship with the lawyer in your life. We hope that you will gain new knowledge, enhance your personal development, and have a more fulfilling relationship with your lawyer. If you are a lawyer yourself, this book will give you insight into your relationships with others.

We know there is no one generalization that characterizes all lawyers. Although you may not find a perfect example of your lawyer, you will certainly find glimpses of him or her scattered throughout these pages.

Chapter 1

Understanding
Your Lawyer

*They have no lawyers among them,
for they consider them as a
sort of people whose profession
it is to disguise matters.*

—Sir Thomas Moore, *Utopia*, 1516

Chapter 1

Understanding Your Lawyer

O ccupational psychology has shown that people with similar personality characteristics tend to gravitate to similar careers. Perhaps you have taken one of those career counseling tests that reveal your interests and aptitudes, and you learned that your personality was best suited for a career as a teacher, a bookkeeper, or a beekeeper. Since similar personality types are best suited for certain professions, it almost appears that the profession develops a life of its own: "He must be an accountant, couldn't you tell by the way he acted?" "She must be a doctor, you know what they are like!" The legal profession is no exception.

Think about the lawyers you know. Regardless of their area of practice, from criminal to environmental, civil to tax, chances are you can think of characteristics they have in common. According to Susan Daicoff, Associate Professor of Law at Florida Coastal Law School, "A review of forty years of empirical research on the psychology of lawyers reveals that, indeed, there is a distinct 'lawyer personality' which distinguishes lawyers from the general population. Some of the traits comprising the lawyer personality appear long before law school, suggesting that those who are suited to practice law self-select into the profession." (Susan Daicoff, "Lawyer, Know Thyself: A Review of Empirical Research on Attorney Attributes Bearing on Professionalism," *The American University Law Review,* June 1997)

This research confirms our experiences and observations over the years that "Yes, Virginia, there is a lawyer personality!" Both male and female lawyers tend to share similar personality characteristics, particularly those expressing satisfaction with their work. In order to understand the unique personality of the lawyer with whom you live, let's first examine what personality is, and where it comes from.

Personality

Personality is the sum of personal attributes that define a person's sense of who (s)he is. In other words, every individual possesses a unique cluster of mental, emotional, social, and physical characteristics which, combined, result in an "inner core." This inner core stays relatively stable. It guides a person's tendency to think, feel, and behave in a consistent manner over time.

Does this inner core come out of the blue? Is it molded in childhood by our parents? Or does it reflect nothing more than a genetic imprint? There are literally volumes of books dedicated solely to answering these questions. However, for the purposes of this book we will give you a brief understanding of the complex interplay of factors that weave together and create the unique fabric that we refer to as "personality."

The term "nature/nurture" refers to the dual importance of that which is innate (nature), and that which is experiential (nurture). Personality is thought to be formed when innate temperament (the biological and genetic disposition with which you are born) interacts with life experiences such as parenting, peer interactions, education, etc. Our life experiences influence our intrinsic capabilities. Nature works in tandem with nurture.

Social scientists often use the metaphor of a computer when attempting to explain the ways in which nature and nurture work together. Nature is the "hardware" of our personality; nurture, the "software."

Nature: The Piece With Which You Are Born

Let's take nature. Nature is the sum total of innate characteristics. Without thinking about it, we all pinpoint someone's nature when we make comments like, "You know how he is" and "That's just like her to do that." Common characteristics thought to be associated with the biological/genetic origins of personality include whether someone tends to be introverted or extroverted, pessimistic or optimistic, rigid or adaptable, logical or emotional, laid back or high-strung. While all of these examples can be affected by the quality and quantity of interactions and experiences a person has in life, it appears that our "central tendency" to be one way or another is largely determined by genetic predisposition. Does this mean we have no choice as to whom we want to be? Hardly! That is where nurture comes into play.

Nurture: The Environmental Influences

Nurture is the sum total of environmental influences that affect the innate temperament of a person. These influences include the amount of love you receive, whether you take piano lessons or play softball, your education, and your religious training. They also include more subtle influences such as the use of alcohol and other drugs, head injuries, and the toxins you breathe. These types of environmental influences affect our brain physiology, thereby altering the nature of our personality.

It is nearly impossible to attribute a certain characteristic to the singular influence of nature or nurture. Researchers have spent years attempting to determine the percentage that each of these, nature and nurture, contribute to the total personality. We've all heard comments such as "Those Smiths are all stubborn!" Is the stubbornness a hardware attribute or a software attribute? Probably both. The genetically determined activity in certain parts of the brain results in a tendency to be stubborn. However, this natural proclivity then interacts with the environment. For example, the Smith children view their parents behaving stubbornly, and model this behavior.

The sum total of a person's nurture experiences will influence each individual depending on the way in which the nature part of their personalities responds to them. No individual will respond the same way. For example, one of the Smith children might express her stubbornness loudly, yelling and screaming along the way, while another might quietly refuse to cooperate by digging in her heels. As Dean Hamer and Peter Copeland put it, "It's part of our nature to respond to nurture." (Dean Hamer and Peter Copeland, *Living with Our Genes: Why They Matter More Than You Think.* Copyright 1998, American Library Assoc.)

O.K., fine and dandy, you say. Just how does all of this relate to lawyers?

The Lawyer Personality

We know that people are happiest and most productive when their interests, strengths, and personality attributes fit with a career that rewards those very interests, strengths and personality attributes. This appears to be the reason research indicates that a certain personality type might gravitate to the practice of law. The legal profession begins to take on a personality of its own, in a way. We are not standing in judgment of that fact. We are merely stating what we have concluded. Our intent is to help you thoroughly understand the nature of the lawyer in your life. Acknowledging and learning about the "lawyer personality" can help both you and your lawyer improve and fully enjoy your relationship.

Know Thy Lawyer

Lawyers tend to share the following traits:

- **Need to achieve**
- **Highly competitive**
- **Articulate**
- **Need to be in control**
- **Problem-solver**
- **Initiator**
- **Cool and aloof**
- **Low Emotional Quotient—E.Q.**
- **Ambitious**
- **Aggressive**
- **High I.Q.**
- **Perfectionist**
- **Defensive**
- **Uncomfortable with intimacy**
- **Passive-aggressive**

These personality traits are encouraged and admired by the legal profession, but at the same time, they can create problems in personal relationships. Certainly, not all of these traits fit every lawyer. However, all lawyers possess *some* combination. Choose the traits that best describe the lawyer in your life and keep that personality in mind as you read this book.

In working with lawyers and their families over the years, there is one general fact that has been conclusively established:

The same characteristics that contribute to the success of a lawyer in the courtroom and in the practice of law are the same characteristics that create problems in the intimate and personal lives of lawyers.

Our book is dedicated to understanding this fact. If people in relationships with lawyers can begin to understand this unique lawyer personality, it is our belief and experience that their relationships will improve. And remember, our research demonstrates that lawyers are less likely to search for understanding of themselves, so somebody is going to have to do it!

The Meyers-Briggs Personality Indicator and the Lawyer Personality

The Meyers-Briggs Personality Indicator is widely used to help people understand their personality type in order to relate and work more effectively with one another. It is a good tool for working with couples to help them understand their differences and styles of communication. We will focus on two of the eight personality types in this tool that we have found to be the most applicable to the lawyer personality. These two personality types are Thinking and Feeling.

If you fall into the Thinking category, you are more likely to be directed by your thoughts, rationale and practicality. For example, you are more likely to buy a car based on price and budget, gas mileage, and insurance options.

If you are predominantly a Feeling person, your emotions, gut reactions, and personal "vibes" govern you. You are more likely to buy a car based on design, color, and comfort level.

People who succeed in the field of law are more likely to fall into the Thinking category. According to Susan J. Bell and Lawrence R. Richard, where a person falls on the Thinking/Feeling scale is the most significant indicator for predicting lawyer satisfaction with his or her job. (Susan J. Bell and Lawrence R. Richard, *Full Disclosure: Do You Really Want to Be a Lawyer? 2nd ed.*) More Feeling types drop out of law school, so we have to wonder if the study and practice of law just isn't compatible with this type of personality.

This Thinking style has been referred to as being reasonable. Certainly many of us have heard that lawyers are of a "reasonable and prudent" nature. You probably have also heard the saying "opposites attract." It is quite common to find that the Thinking lawyer has chosen to be in a relationship with a predominantly Feeling partner. When the reasonable and prudent lawyers live and relate on a daily basis with intuitive and spontaneous people, misunderstanding and misinterpretations occur quite frequently. This does not have to become a problem, if each partner recognizes that (s)he is experiencing the world very differently from the other's point of view. In fact, the Meyers-Briggs Personality Indicator suggests that opposite types are best suited for long-term, intimate relationships, and reports a high success rate. Similar personality types tend to be best suited for friendships and show a less successful rate for intimate relationships over a long period of time.

Just a Joke

Q: How can you spot a law student on a large university campus?
A: Even on a semi-cloudy day, they all carry umbrellas.

What Your Lawyer Has Learned

If we consider personality traits the "nature" of the lawyer, then what lawyers learn in law school makes up the "nurture" component of the picture. Do not confuse "nurture" here with nurturing. Law schools, in and of themselves, are not nurturing environments. But they *do* represent the environment in which all lawyers "grow up" professionally.

Lawyers are trained to perform in certain ways. Legal training prepares your lawyer to "fight to win," among other strategies. They become verbal gladiators. Male and female lawyers alike prepare to become knights in that very prestigious and exclusive club known as King Arthur's Court. They learn to joust with each other by joking sarcastically, and practice fighting each other in moot court. They often isolate themselves from those who are not preparing to become noble knights of that great round table by eating, drinking, playing, and studying together.

Lawyers are trained to do the following:

- **Cross-examine**
- **Doubt others**
- **Speak for others**
- **Win the point**
- **Stonewall, outwit, hinder & delay**
- **Argue every point**
- **Think for others**
- **Manipulate the facts**
- **Avoid errors**
- **Never show weakness**

When a lawyer uses these tactics in the courtroom, (s)he succeeds. When a lawyer uses these tactics at home, problems arise. The diagram below shows how these "legal" lessons interfere with intimate and social relationships.

Successful Lawyer Techniques	Successful Relationship Techniques
Cross-examine	Have a give and take discussion
Argue every point	Listen and decide if the point is worth arguing
Doubt others	Trust others
Think for others	Respect partner's own opinions and ideas
Speak for others	Allow equal time for partner's input
Manipulate the facts	Be honest
Avoid errors	Admit mistakes
Win the point	Compromise
Never show weakness	Allow yourself to be vulnerable
Stonewall, outwit, hinder & delay	Cooperate with your partner

It doesn't take much to see that the left and right sides of the above are truly diametrically opposed.

Did you know your lawyer before (s)he went to law school? If you did, you likely noticed how much (s)he changed during those four-odd years. People who watch others go through law school are often amazed at the changes they witness. We often hear "He seems like a different person," "She is always arguing with me," and, "He sounds just like a lawyer."

Law school is unlike any other education. It is the start of a person's entry into the exclusive society of "The Attorney." Law school puts a group of aspiring professionals together for several years to experience intensely stressful circumstances. Law students form a common bond as they learn new ways to think, act, and even feel. Benjamin Sells makes the following observations about law students:

> The law student is becoming more argumentative over the least little thing, almost seeming to look for a chance to argue; they have become a little haughty, assuming an air of superiority; they seem older, as if they are trying to affect a range of experience beyond their years; or they are simply not as much fun as they used to be....The simple fact is that there appears to be something about law school that disconnects people from the life they had before. (Benjamin Sells, *The Soul of the Law*, Element, Rockport, MA: 1994)

If you add these two pieces together—the nature of the lawyer's personality and the nurture of the law school experience—the result is too often the following:

The nature of the lawyer's personality

+ The nurture of the law school experience

Professional success in the field of law but unhappiness and a lack of fulfillment in personal life

---

Of course, this equation is not always the result, but it is valuable information if you attempt to understand this unique breed.

HOW LAWYERS DIFFER FROM THE GENERAL POPULATION

In Early Childhood	As Pre-Law Students	Effects of Law School	As Lawyers
1. Scholastic achievement orientation, reading.			Need for achievement.
2. Leadership, authoritarian male dominance emphasis. Active approach to life, emphasis on self-discipline instead of submission to authority.	Need for dominance, leadership, and attention. Less subordinate and deferent, more authoritarian.	Increased aggression and ambition when under stress. Preference for competitive peer relations, failure to rely on peers for social support.	Extroversion and sociability. Competitiveness, masculinity, argumentativeness, aggression, dominance, coldness, tendency to quarrel, disagreeable.
3. Low interest in emotions or concern for others' feelings.	Low interest in emotions, interpersonal concerns, and others' feelings.	Increased "rights" focus (justice, rationality, etc.) as opposed to an "ethic of care."	Low interest in people, emotional concerns, and interpersonal matters; disproportionate preference for "Thinking" vs. "Feeling;" conventional, rules/rights-based morality.
4. Authors' note: No data available.	Higher socioeconomic status; materialistic motives.	Decreased interest in public interest work; increased interest in private practice.	Materialism; focus on economic bottom line.
5. Authors' note: No data available.	Normal levels of psychological distress.	Increased psychological distress and substance abuse, increased tension and insecurity.	Higher incidence of psychological distress and substance abuse; pessimistic outlook on life.

Justice is Served: A Case Study

John, a lawyer, and Laura, his wife, entered therapy at Laura's request. Laura was feeling anger and disappointment with her marriage. She said the problems started while John was in law school. Law school absorbed all of his time and emotional energy. He was never able to find enough time to be with her. After graduation, John took a job with a large law firm, and for a while she believed things would get better. Now that John was a practicing attorney and not just a struggling student, their lives would become "more normal."

Needless to say, that was not the case. As an ambitious lawyer, John was always looking forward to the next step up. His drive for perfection caused him to work late hours as he racked up billable hours. He brought work home on weekends and his competitive nature pressured him to always attend the firm's happy hours. Like many of his colleagues, he became involved in community and political organizations during his "free" time. Laura began to resent these intrusions into their private time. Then, John received a promotion that involved more intense cases and travel out of town. John was always promising Laura that "as soon as this case is over, I will have more time to be with you at home." But another case always came along, leaving Laura feeling even more lonely.

John's career star was rising, and he began to make a good deal of money. They bought a large home in an

affluent community and lived well, yet Laura still wasn't happy.
John had good intentions of spending time with his wife, but
when he did get home for dinner he was usually exhausted from
the stress of his job. Laura's asking for more of John's time
began to feel like nagging to John and he began to stay even
later at the office. When he was home, he found himself feeling
angry and argumentative. They fought often.

As the couple went through therapy, they realized they really did
love each other and were committed to their relationship. How could
they have drifted so far apart, arguing over every little thing? What
happened to make this relationship so unfulfilling?

In couples' therapy, they gained insight into John's typical Lawyer
Personality: Win at all costs, climb the law firm's ladder of success,
and be ambitious, ambitious, ambitious!

As Laura began to understand the unique aspects of her spouse's
personality, she was able to empathize with John. She admitted she had
unrealistic expectations about his schedule and adjusted her irrational
beliefs. She realized that much of her nagging was really a **demand**
that John put her before his law practice. She discovered she had
become oblivious to the fact that she was enjoying some of the results
of John's hard work and his ambitious nature. After taking herself out
of "competition" with the law, Laura regained her sense of self and
continued taking responsibility for her own happiness. She was able to
stop trying to change John and became more confident and relaxed
with herself.

And, as she let go of her anxiety, John was able to better understand that Laura's biggest complaint was that he was never really there—listening, in the moment, enjoying his wife. He discovered that taking a few minutes to really listen to Laura, so that she felt understood and validated, strengthened their relationship. He also learned to share his own feelings, and to get past his lawyer attributes of being uncomfortable with intimacy and having difficulty identifying his own feelings.

As a result of Laura's growth and a "softer" approach to John, he became more sensitive to her needs, learned to identify his own feelings, and even respected Laura's decision to seek therapeutic help.

And, how did all of these changes occur? Laura was able to let John know that her complaints were because she really cared and wanted to have a more intimate relationship with him. That is what this book is about...finding ways to empower yourself to have a more fulfilling relationship with your lawyer.

Just a Joke

Q: How many lawyers does it take to screw in a light bulb?
A: One—the lawyer holds it while the rest of the world revolves around him.

4 Benefits of Living With Your Lawyer

1. Clout by association. Have a customer complaint? Wondering if your car mechanic is scamming you? Use the magic words, "I will have my spouse, who is a lawyer, give you a call..."

2. Free legal advice. Being able to get legal advice anytime, without having to pay a billable hourly rate (at least we hope you don't get billed...).

3. Lawyers are predictable, so you can usually count on their habitual patterns not changing. Therefore, their behavior becomes the yardstick by which you can measure your own progress and growth.

4. Lawyers are great in an emotional crisis. They provide a steady, stable and rational perspective.

Just a Joke

Q: What's wrong with lawyer jokes?

A: Lawyers don't think they're funny and other people don't think they're jokes.

Boss, Your Traits Are Showing

At seminars held for legal secretaries, the question "What are the aspects of working for a lawyer that cause you the most stress?" was posed. The most common answers below illustrate the image of the lawyer personality and how it affects the secretaries with whom lawyers live on a daily basis in the workplace:

- "Lawyers are always right about everything— even when they are not."
- "Lawyers never admit to making a mistake."
- "Lawyers feel that everyone else is beneath them."
- "Lawyers are inflexible and refuse to change their ways."
- "Lawyers aren't easy to approach when you have a question."
- "Lawyers don't appreciate what other people do for them."
- "Lawyers expect you to drop everything and do what they want you to do."
- "Lawyers have big egos."

Chapter 2

Never Argue
With A Lawyer

COMMUNICATION DYNAMICS

*It is the trade of lawyers
to question everything,
yield nothing, and
to talk by the hour.*

—Thomas Jefferson

---- *Chapter 2* ----

Never Argue
With A Lawyer

COMMUNICATION DYNAMICS

Communicating with another person is not always easy because it involves sharing your personal, emotional, and intimate self. It can be even harder when you are communicating with a lawyer. Lawyers are very articulate and skilled communicators. They are trained to be mouthpieces and to speak for others. They are trained to argue, negotiate, and to win their point. Toss in their egos, and talking to a lawyer can be intimidating, to say the least.

It is critical to remember that the lawyer has been trained to communicate within the legal system. These strategies are diametrically opposed to creating intimacy in a relationship, and interfere with empowering the listener's sense of self-respect. If you don't understand the underlying source of this communication style, you are likely to get your feelings hurt and lose your sense of self.

Let's face it—you are the underdog in a conversation with your lawyer. The communication techniques your lawyer has learned can leave you feeling frustrated, patronized, helpless, and out of control. However, recognizing how lawyers communicate and ways to respond to them can help you hold your own. We'll look at a few ways to respond when you have just been hit by the steam-roller tactics that are so effective in a courtroom argument—and so harmful to a relationship.

Court is now in session.

Just the Facts, Ma'am, Just the Facts: Communicating With Your Lawyer

The goal of communication is for the *intent* of the speaker to match the *impact* the message has on the listener. When the intent and the impact match, we feel close to, understood by, and inti-mate with the other person. On the other hand, when the intent and the impact are very different, we feel as if we are miles apart. For example, if I intend to communicate that I am frustrated, but the listener hears that I am blaming her for my frustration, the communication is not going to be successful. Miscommunication is like two actors on the same stage, reciting lines from two different plays. Each actor has his own agenda and the messages are not communicated or understood clearly. You are likely to have experienced this at one time or another.

Communication is a process that involves people taking two main roles: the listener and the speaker. The following are guidelines for you, the non-lawyer, to practice facilitating the communication with the lawyer in your life.

Guidelines for Becoming an Effective Speaker

The speaker is the person who is in control of the conversation. Lawyers do not like to let each other speak, let alone listen to a non-lawyer. Remember those traits: Articulate! Verbal Gladiators! Lawyers often are referred to as "mouthpieces." This is not a negative characteristic for an attorney; in fact, it is what people pay them to do. As such, they are not always the best listeners. Their intelligent minds are often moving way ahead. So when you speak, you need to get your message across in a way that your lawyer can most effectively process and understand. Follow these guidelines when speaking to your lawyer.

- **Know what you want before you express your thought to your partner. Do not be wishy-washy.**

- **Get to the point. Lawyers hate it when you waste their time with too many words. Know your bottom line and keep it short and sweet.**

- **Understand the intention behind your words. Ask yourself, "What is the message I want to be heard?" Lawyers do not like to guess at what you mean. If you are unclear, they become impatient.**

- **State your message articulately. As we have noted, lawyers tend to be naturally articulate and they respect others who have this skill.**

- **Use I-statements to avoid sounding as if you are blaming or attacking the other person. An I-statement is a phrase spoken in the first person focusing on your own feelings and not those of the other person. I-statements are empowering to the speaker so (s)he does not sound like a victim. Example: "I am angry" as opposed to "You make me angry."**

- **Be aware of your nonverbal messages, including your tone of voice, posture, gestures, and level of pitch. Good lawyers notice nonverbal signs. In the courtroom they can "read" jury members' nonverbal responses to their arguments, at the negotiation table they can tell who is going to give in, and when talking to a client, they can often tell who is lying.**

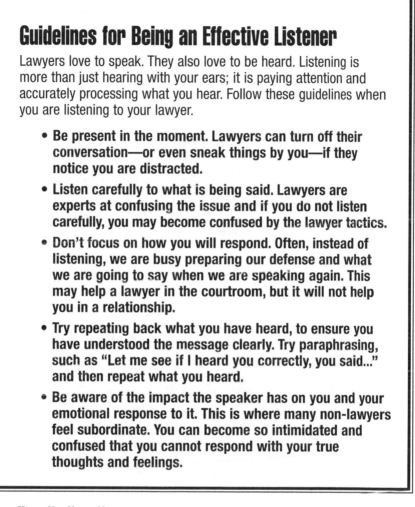

Guidelines for Being an Effective Listener

Lawyers love to speak. They also love to be heard. Listening is more than just hearing with your ears; it is paying attention and accurately processing what you hear. Follow these guidelines when you are listening to your lawyer.

- **Be present in the moment. Lawyers can turn off their conversation—or even sneak things by you—if they notice you are distracted.**
- **Listen carefully to what is being said. Lawyers are experts at confusing the issue and if you do not listen carefully, you may become confused by the lawyer tactics.**
- **Don't focus on how you will respond. Often, instead of listening, we are busy preparing our defense and what we are going to say when we are speaking again. This may help a lawyer in the courtroom, but it will not help you in a relationship.**
- **Try repeating back what you have heard, to ensure you have understood the message clearly. Try paraphrasing, such as "Let me see if I heard you correctly, you said..." and then repeat what you heard.**
- **Be aware of the impact the speaker has on you and your emotional response to it. This is where many non-lawyers feel subordinate. You can become so intimidated and confused that you cannot respond with your true thoughts and feelings.**

Hear Ye, Hear Ye

You can practice learning to listen to each other by choosing a low-conflict issue. The designated speaker holds a TV remote control clicker, which indicates that (s)he is in control of the conversation at that moment. We all know that the person who holds the clicker is indeed in control! There is no interruption, as only the person with the clicker is allowed to speak. The speaker discusses an issue, short and to the point. The listener then paraphrases what (s)he has heard. The clicker is then passed on to the listener, and the roles are reversed. You will be amazed at how difficult this simple task is.

The Filtering System

The filtering system is one of the most significant barriers to effective communication. It is often the culprit for the message being misinterpreted by the listener. For example, when you were a kid, you might have played the game called Telephone, long before e-mail, voice mail and cell phones. One person, at the beginning of the row, would whisper something to the kid sitting behind her. The second kid would then whisper to the kid behind her, and continue until the message reached the last kid in the row. The last kid would then say the statement out loud. Rarely did the message make it the whole way down the aisle without a mix-up! There is not likely to be a whole row of real, live people between you and your lawyer when you are communicating with each other, but there are factors that alter what you hear just as if there were. These factors are called filters. They trigger an emotional response when heard. Sometimes your filter is a scripted message, or a tone of voice, or words usually connected to your childhood experiences. For example, a filter might be an irrational belief or thought, illustrated in the following exchange:

- *Lawyer speaker says* to his wife getting dressed in the early morning: "Do I have any clean underwear?"
- *Filtering system:* Belief that a good wife should always have laundry caught up and put away. Remember, we said that filters can be irrational beliefs. Therefore,
- *Listener Wife hears:* "What is the matter with you that you did not get the laundry done?"
- *Result = Hurt feelings leading to anger and her angry response,* "Am I supposed to do everything around here?"

Note that the message heard is way off from the message sent.

- *Lawyer speaker says* (to his wife): "I am going to stop after work with some folks and discuss this case."
- *Filtering system:* When she was a child, her father was a workaholic and never spent time with his family. The accompanying myth is that if a man really loves his wife, he wants to come straight home when the workday is done and share everything with her.

- *Listener hears:* "I'd rather be with my friends than home with you." And also, "You don't understand these things like my lawyer friends do!" (The last statement, by the way, is true! You do not understand just like his or her lawyer friends. And that is O.K.) Nevertheless, the
- *Result = Hurt feelings leading to anger.*

A suggestion here is for you, the non-lawyer in this duo, to increase self-awareness and become familiar with your own filtering process so you can be in charge of your reactions. Your responses will then be less emotional and more rational, which lawyers like, remember? Those lovable, reasonable and prudent creatures!

At Ease With Legalese

Does this sound familiar? You are at a dinner party full of lawyers and their significant others. The lawyers are sitting around comparing battle scars, laughing, and having a good old time. The significant others sit silently with glazed expressions on their faces. "I'd join in the conversation," the non-lawyers think, "if I could understand what the heck they are talking about." Tort feasers! De facto! Mea culpa! Who can blame us for feeling left out? It certainly isn't that we non-lawyers are any less intelligent or socially skilled than our lawyers. Yet, a major filter that can interfere with your conversations with lawyers is that they have learned a foreign language—legal jargon, or "legalese."

The legal terms lawyers use in law school carry over into their everyday conversations. Using legal jargon alienates those of us outside the legal profession. It can make you feel uncomfortable, patronized, and frankly, bored. The best way to deal with this? If you can't beat them, join them. Learn the lingo. Study up on legal termi-nology by skimming a law dictionary. Carry a pocket size one with you or, if you are techno-savvy, look them up quickly at an online dictionary (locate a list of online legal dictionaries at http://www.Johannaalaw.com.) If you have the interest, read law journals and web sites and really wow them with your knowledge.

Remember: You are not a defendant. You are not a client. You are not a witness.

The Courtroom vs. The Living Room

In a trial, each side is permitted to question the other side's witnesses. This is called cross-examination. The goal of cross-examination might be to discredit someone or to get into evidence that which is positive for your case. Cross-examining involves asking questions that already suggest an answer, such as "It is sunny outside, isn't that true?" Cross-examination is the single most important skill for any litigator to master. It takes a great deal of preparation and experience to become proficient at it.

If you live with a lawyer, you most likely find yourself being cross-examined as if you were on the witness stand, testifying for the opposition. It is important to recognize your lawyer's tendency to cross-examine. If you don't, you fall into the trap of agreeing with all of the lawyer's leading questions. Being cross-examined is not a pleasant experience, and one in which you usually will not prevail.

James W. McElhaney of Case Western University School of Law identified six "rules of the road" for cross-examination. However, these rules can interfere with communication outside the courtroom.

1. *Ask only leading questions. The point of cross-examination is not to get information from the witness, but to have the witness agree that what you say is true.* This rule is a great courtroom strategy, but it doesn't take much effort to see that if the word witness is replaced with, say, "wife," the duo is headed for problems.

2. *Ask short questions. Make questions disarmingly short, such as "This is a letter to Mr. Wells? Offering to sell you a patent? Written by you? On your stationery?"* Questions like these do not give the respondent any wiggle room— which is exactly what your lawyer intends. Is it any wonder that people living with lawyers are heard to say, "I feel like I am on the witness stand"? This rule will block intimacy.

3. *Your job is to command instant comprehension. Be merciless with yourself. Get rid of convoluted, sesquipedalian, tergiversation that makes you sound like a lawyer.* While some of this rule can be helpful to create intimacy and understanding, the words "command instant" certainly are not. The part about a lawyer being merciless to himself could be helpful; maybe not necessarily merciless, just aware. After all, you would certainly prefer that your lawyer not sound like, well, a lawyer, when talking to you. This is especially true when (s)he is dealing with your feelings.

4. *Do not start questions with phrases such as "Let me ask you this question," "Isn't it a fact that..." "It is true, isn't it now?" and end with statements such as "Isn't it correct?" "Isn't that so?" or "That's true, isn't it?" Introductions and endings like these are simply verbal clutter that dilute what you are saying with unnecessary sound.* From an intimacy perspective, the downside is: the manner in which the questions are asked—the tone of cross-examination—does not create an environment in which you feel safe to share your feelings. The content of the question has the goal of getting you to agree. Recognize this. For creating intimacy, the upside is: it might not be verbal clutter to begin with a statement such as "Let me ask you a question so I can get your advice." This technique can work to state your need directly prior to making a statement so that your intention is clear up front, and to avoid misinterpretations.

5. *Ask for facts and not opinions. Good cross-examiners avoid using modifiers—adjectives and adverbs—because they invite witnesses to give their opinions.* In your personal relationship with your lawyer, the reverse is true. You want your lawyer to ask for and respect your opinions. Be aware that a lawyer in cross-examination mode does not want your opinion, and (s)he certainly has no regard for your feelings. Remember, juries are instructed to find evidence based on fact, not on their feelings or gut reactions. When your lawyer uses this rule in conversation with you, it is hard to imagine that your feelings are being valued.

6. *Get one fact at a time. Think of cross-examination as a series of little fact-dots that the judge and jury will connect in their minds. Your picture then becomes their idea. And because it is their idea, they believe in it.*

This is the rule that, when used in personal communication, leaves you feeling you have been manipulated—and indeed you have been! (James W. McElhaney, "Make it Habit-Forming," *ABA Journal,* June 1998)

Remind yourself that your lawyer has been trained to argue and to win. This will help you avoid taking this style too personally. This awareness is your key to avoid being "buffaloed" so to speak, backed into a corner and intimidated.

On the Witness Stand: A Case Study

William is a criminal defense attorney. Much of his practice takes place in the courtroom attempting to discredit prosecution witnesses. His wife, Teresa, is a teacher who wants to buy new school clothes for their two children. The couple had the following discussion:

William:	*"So you say that the children need new school clothes."*
Teresa:	*"Yes."*
William:	*"The kids have not grown much since last year, right?"*
Teresa:	*"Yes, not much."*
William:	*"You take good care of the kids' clothes, right?"*
Teresa:	*"Yes."*
William:	*"So the kids haven't grown and the clothes are in good shape. So, they don't need new school clothes, right?"*
Teresa:	*(Reluctantly) "I guess."*

Clearly, Teresa realizes she is having a problem getting her point across to William. His style is intimidating to her. Again, a good lawyering tactic—intimidating opposing counsel. Since William practices his cross-examination on her almost daily, he is not likely to change his habits. Teresa is going to have to find a way to avoid falling into William's cross-examination trap.

To respond to William's communication style, Teresa needs to learn the following:

- Avoid using only the words "yes" and "no" in her answers to his questions. The one word answer is what your lawyer desires from the person on the witness stand, ("Please, just answer yes or no."), but it does not help you when you are trying to take a stand at the kitchen sink.

- Be prepared. Lawyers are trained to always be prepared. So be prepared, too. Practice an anticipated discussion, talk the conversation through in the car, at the office, or while working out. Listen to your tone and be prepared to stand by your convictions.

- Use humor to deal with your reasonable and prudent lawyer. Lighten up the situation. Lawyers need more humor; the law is a serious business. They often appreciate your being "light" in your discussions with them.

For example, Teresa might have tried a touch of humor, which might have thrown William off a little. "Let me see if I heard you correctly: You are being so sensitive and understanding, and do not want me to spend more than $500 on each kid, right?" Or, "You may be right. I guess Johnny could wear Susie's hand-me-downs this year. Let's see, her purple bell-bottoms, her plaid skirt...."

Now, since Teresa has read this book, let's replay the conversation more effectively. Look at Teresa's new rebuttal.

William:	*"So you say that the children need new school clothes."*
Teresa:	*"Yes, that's a fact."*
William:	*"The kids have not grown much since last year, right?"*
Teresa:	*"Yes, not much, but enough to be in the next size."*
William:	*"You take good care of the kids' clothes, right?"*

Teresa:	"Yes, and good enough care so I can donate them and we'll get a tax write-off."
William:	"So the kids haven't grown much and the clothes are in good shape. So, they don't need new school clothes, right?"
Teresa:	(Smiling) "You're right. They don't need a whole new wardrobe. However, they do need some new clothes. It will probably cost about $150 per child."
William:	Being his reasonable and prudent self..."O.K., that sounds reasonable and will probably fit into the budget."

Since Teresa didn't get caught up in William's cross-examination style, the result is much better for her.

The Lawyer's Appeal

Having someone around who is skilled in cross-examination is not always a negative, If it is not being used against you. You and your lawyer can both learn to use cross-examination techniques for good, not evil. While cross-examining you, the lawyer can play devil's advocate and point out views you might not have considered. This can result in your seeing the situation from a different, perhaps more enlightened, perspective.

The Attack on Intimacy

When you are living with a lawyer, sooner or later you are bound to have an argument. All couples fight. Most of them, however, don't fight like the couples in which one partner is a lawyer. Lawyers have spent at least three years and serious tuition money learning to fight to the death. Lawyers take no prisoners in an argument. They have to win, win, win at all costs. It doesn't matter if you are fighting about buying a new house or ordering take-out. Most likely, your lawyer won't give up until (s)he sits victoriously in a suburban colonial home, eating his chicken lo mein. You, on the other hand, are left only with your fond dreams of a house in the country, a craving for a burger with fries, and a heavy heart.

It is very likely that your lawyer is highly skilled at turning the tables on you in a discussion or disagreement. Somewhere in the process, you suddenly realize that (s)he has made everything appear to be your fault. You are being blamed, you are in the wrong, you are the bad guy. And you are under attack. You even find yourself feeling guilty or ashamed, even though, at the start of the discussion, you were sure you were in the right. You wonder, "How did this happen?" Often this awareness comes too late to avoid the hurt you feel. Whoever said, "Sticks and stones can break my bones but words will never hurt me" had likely never been in an argument with a lawyer!

We asked a group of spouses of lawyers for the definition of feeling hurt. Their responses include:

- "You feel sad and depressed."

- "You are devalued, and the hurt is deep and personal."

- "You want to cry and often do, but you also are angry."

In therapy, the author helps patients identify the hurt, which often is really the feeling of anger turned inward—and then learn to release it. The original hurt does not actually cause the lasting damage to you or the relationship. It is the "hanging on" to the hurt that creates the problem. So knowing that your lawyer is trained to wound you when (s)he attacks, be prepared to feel the hurt, identify it, breathe deeply, and then let it go. You might even find something to deflect him/her, such as finding something in the criticism with which you agree. Try saying, "You are right, at least about how you feel."

Remember this fact: In personal relationships, the lawyer who is attacking you is an anxious one. If you know that, it somehow hurts less. Try your own self-defense by saying to yourself, "(S)he really needed to say that for whatever reason. That does not mean

that I needed to hear it." Again, breathe in slowly and exhale for as
long as you can. Get rid of those poisons of hurt and anger.

---

*Author's note: It is not healthy to remain in a truly verbally abusive
relationship. The author is referring throughout this book to a normal
lawyer-like style, not to incidents where those lawyer traits are so
severe that they are pathological. If you believe you are being
abused, or if alcohol is at the root of these attacks, seek professional
help immediately.*

**Make requests and not demands. Requests are flattering and
usually more likely to be fulfilled. Demands are challenging and
often resisted. Remember, lawyers always feel they have to
meet a challenge and win. Challenge them and you are in
for the duration!**

Just a Joke

Q: How do you know when a lawyer is lying?
A: His lips move.

Problem Discussion vs. Problem Solving

Often, when you communicate at a personal or intimate level,
all you really want is to be heard, understood and have your
thoughts and feelings affirmed. This process is called problem
discussion. However, the trained legal mind processes conversations differently. A lawyer begins to immediately try to solve your
perceived problem and offer a solution. This is called problem
solving. These are two very different processes. Problem solving is
a lawyer's trade. This is what you want when you hire an attorney.
Problem discussion is a loving partner's trade. This is what you
want when you need understanding and affirmation—someone to
listen to you and be emotionally supportive.

Mistrial: A Case Study

Aliyah is married to Everett, who has recently started his first job out of law school. She is frustrated with his late work hours. She tells him, "You never come home for dinner, you don't care about me." Everett's response is "Why do you think I work so hard and can't come home sometimes—so I can take care of you. I'll just grab fast food for my dinner, so don't worry about me."

Aliyah wanted to be heard, understood, and have her feelings validated. Her husband's response did none of those things. He indicated he was working late for her, so he felt her feelings were invalid. She felt even more misunderstood, hurt, and confused about her desire to spend more time with her husband. Had he responded with empathy for her feelings, such as "You're feeling like I really don't care about our relationship because I work so late? I can see why you might feel that way," we can guarantee she would have felt heard, understood, and would not have believed that her feelings must be wrong because they were so quickly dismissed.

Reminder: This is not a book about how to change the lawyer in your life, and you are not likely to get that emotionally supportive response from him or her. But, if you are able to change some of your own ways of communicating, then the lawyer in your life just might change a bit in response.

In this case, the wife really did not expect that the husband would suddenly come home for dinner every night. However, we cannot blame him for jumping to his solution of the perceived problem due to the way it was communicated. Just the same, he missed the real issue—it was not about dinner; she was feeling unimportant and unloved.

If you present a problem to your lawyer, expect a solution. Lawyers are good at that. In the Mistrial case study, the wife was not clear about what she really wanted. Often you may know what you do not want, but you may not really be clear about what you do want. To prevent the confusion of problem solving and problem discussion, try the following strategies:

> Identify when you want to have a discussion about the problem versus a problem solving session. You can prevent your lawyer from prematurely jumping in with a solution by stating up front, "All I need from you, at this moment, is for you to hear me and listen, and hopefully understand what is going on with me."

> Also, tell your lawyer up front that this will not take hours; what you need is just a few moments. Then choose to be satisfied with the time you've shared.

> Be as brief and concise as possible. Your lawyer may very well have difficulty understanding the value of simply listening to understand, without solving the problem. This is especially true if (s)he is anticipating that this means a discussion about your feelings. Remember that lawyers have a low E.Q. (emotional quotient) and indeed may even find a discussion about feelings a waste of time.

So, if you want emotional support, tell your lawyer. You may also need to explain to him or her what that means. So know what you want! Be direct. For example, emotionally supportive behavior can be as simple as giving a hug or holding you while you cry. Or allowing you to vent your anger without your lawyer getting defensive or trying to talk you out of your feelings with rational thoughts. Tell him or her exactly what you want.

Reinforce when your lawyer does respond in a way you like, perhaps by saying "Thank you, I really appreciate that you listened to me." It never hurts the cause to reinforce desired behavior. Lawyers, like all of us, need to know they are appreciated. Unfortunately, too often, the lawyers' significant others fail to provide this appreciation.

Motive vs. Behavior

Note to lawyers! When your significant other is sharing feelings with you, never ask "why" she is feeling the way she is feeling. Just as with the practice of law, a motive behind the behavior is not as important as the facts. Her feelings are fact. They are real facts and do not need a rational basis. They just are!

As a lawyer, you know that motive is not as important as the alleged illegal behavior on trial. Why one commits a crime is not as important as whether or not a client is guilty or innocent of that crime. And although the motive behind the behavior might sometimes be relevant, it is important that you stick to the facts.

Knowing why does not change the fact. Knowing why your spouse is angry does not change the fact that she is, indeed, angry. Knowing why does not solve the problem, especially if you perceive that her having feelings is the problem and you just want it to go away. Her anger will disappear more quickly if you just listen and do not question it. Knowing why does not change anything. Many people know why they smoke or overeat, but knowing why does not magically make it easy to not smoke or overeat.

Also, in a personal conversation, "why" questions generally leave the recipients of the question feeling like they have done something wrong. Take this parenting example:

Dad comes home from work and finds his five-year-old's bicycle sitting in the middle of the driveway so that he cannot get his car into the garage. Dad goes into the house and asks his son, "Tommy, why did you leave the bike in the driveway?" We guarantee you that Tommy does not have the slightest notion as to why he left it there—he forgot...he was just going to be in the house a little while...he was getting ready to go out...none of the "why's" really matter. What Tommy hears is that Dad is angry and Tommy did something wrong.

Have Your Lawyer Read This

Listening and affirming your loved one's feelings, without questioning them, and letting them know you understand, can be a wonderful gift to give your relationship.

Editing

Just as the editor carefully edited the words in this book, you can learn to edit what you are saying to your lawyer. Choose your words carefully and think before you speak. Before you speak, you hold the power. After you speak, the power is in the words. Editing is a smart choice that one makes not to always "tell it like it is." Do you really need to tell the truth, the whole truth, and nothing but the truth? Sometimes what you think of as honesty is actually criticism that is mean and hurtful. Yes, honesty is a virtue, but you do not have to process truth in such a raw form that it blocks intimacy.

You can also edit how you choose to hear someone else, and you can choose how you are going to respond.

Innocent Until Decided Guilty: Case Study

A retired corporate lawyer and his wife, both in their seventies and married close to fifty years, sought professional advice in regard to their grandson. During this process, it became evident that this couple had a wonderful intimate relationship with each other. When asked what they thought might be the main dynamic responsible for their successful and long-lasting marriage, the wife responded immediately. "Oh that is easy," she said. "Before we were even married, I decided to create a list of ten things that really annoyed me about him. And then I decided I would just ignore those ten things when he did them, and focus on the things I really liked." She continued that when he did or said those annoying things, she would ignore them or dismiss them with little thought. "After all," she said, "my father said that you might not be able to help it if a bird lands on your head, but you do not have to build a nest for it." So she had decided when an annoyance surfaced in her marriage, she was not going to foster it.

When asked what those ten annoying things were, she replied, "Oh, I don't know! I never got around to making that list. But every time he did something that frustrated me I would say to myself: Oh boy, is he ever lucky that it is one of those ten things I said I would never let bother me!"

This is a wonderful demonstration that it was not the behavior that was annoying, but what she chose to tell herself about the behavior that determined how she felt and therefore was able to respond. See Chapter 5, Belief System: Rational vs. Irrational, for more on this dynamic.

The words "smart choice" were used in describing the editing process. The fact is, you choose how to process and respond to what your lawyer says. This is an important dynamic that goes unnoticed much of the time. When you know it is indeed your choice, you are then in control and not merely reacting to the lawyer's words automatically and without thought. When you choose how you are going to respond to someone else's words and behaviors, you are more in control of your own happiness.

The very wise woman in the Innocent Until Decided Guilty scenario was in control over how she interpreted her lawyer's behavior. She was not a poor victim; she was a victor because she made choices that strengthened her relationship while keeping a healthy attitude about herself. Early in the relationship she chose what she was going to do. As a result, his behavior was secondary to her response to his behavior. **This does not mean she was secondary to him.** It means she was not simply reacting to him, but choosing how to respond. Preparing your conversations and responses in advance is one way to keep control over them. The author of this book actually does this when she is in her car:

> *"While I am driving my car, I talk out loud to myself. It is a time when I can be alone and sort out what I really want to communicate to my husband. Since the invention of car phones, I no longer get strange looks from other drivers who see me talking to myself. I focus on getting my message across succinctly and in the right tone. I remind myself to get to the bottom line, as attorneys do not like to waste words. I find it helps to talk out loud, so I can hear the tone of my voice. I find myself saying things like, 'I do not need to say all that,' 'What do I want him to know about this issue,' and 'What do I need to say in order to feel better?' By the time I have edited it out for myself, it usually is quite a good message. In fact, I often find that after a driving conversation with myself, I do not even need to bring up the issue with my husband. It sometimes gets resolved through my self-talk."*

When you understand your reaction and consciously choose how you are going to respond, or what decision you are going to make, you are empowered. You don't need the other person to change.

Communicating for Intimacy vs. Control

Often, when you communicate your unhappiness or anger to your lawyer, what you really want is for him or her to change so that you no longer feel the way you do. For example, you might be unhappy that your lawyer is immersed in a case and seems to only think about work when (s)he is home. You plan to talk to your lawyer about your feelings, hoping that once (s)he knows you are unhappy and feeling neglected (s)he will change the behavior.

Communicating your feelings because you really want and expect your lawyer to change empowers your lawyer. You are stuck with your feelings still trapped inside if (s)he does not respond with what you want. You will ultimately feel victimized and feel more and more out of control.

On the other hand, when you share your feelings simply to share closeness and become more intimate, you are the one in control. You are not trying to control the other person's response. Communicating for intimacy is healthier in a relationship. You cannot expect your partner to change a behavior just because you say you don't like it. Now, that is not to say that would not be nice. It is just not realistic, and not necessary. If you desire intimacy in your relationship with your lawyer, then the agenda cannot be about control. Rather, intimacy is about sharing your feelings and innermost thoughts and knowing that although you are vulnerable, you are willing to take that risk and then feel good about taking it. Regardless of the result.

Of course, this is easier said than done. It is not being

suggested, here, that any of these things are simple to do for yourself. There are times when we all want to control our environment and the people around us. Sometimes it is hard not to become controlling, and not to get into a power struggle with a loved one. It is only human to want approval and validation from others. The problem? It never works!

Case Closed: A Case Study

James is a lawyer and a perfect role model for those aspiring to have the lawyer personality attributes for winning cases. James always had to be in control. He also described himself as a man with a "one-track mind," but believed that was an attribute that helped make him successful in his profession. However, James was frustrated because he and his wife were constantly getting into power struggles. In counseling, James reported a recent power struggle that had occurred between he and his wife. He told the following story:

He and Maggie were packing for a ski trip to Colorado. They both loved to ski and were in great spirits. Maggie thought aloud as they packed, "How would you like to skip a day of skiing and try parasailing off the mountain during this trip?" James immediately responded, "What a stupid idea." Maggie regained her composure after being hit hard with such a criticism and said, "I heard it was kind of fun." James retorted, "We don't have time for that. We are going on a ski trip. On a ski trip, you ski. Not fool around with para-crap." Maggie then said, "I just heard it was fun, that's all." James's reply was "It is stupid and would be a waste of our time. And that is that." Maggie didn't speak to him the rest of the time they were packing.

The psychologist listened carefully and after James finished his story, she shared with James the following scene she had personally witnessed:

I was waiting for a flight at the airport, watching the people hurrying to their planes. The airport was quite busy and crowded. Most people move through airports very quickly. So it was with a young pregnant woman who was hurrying along the crowded walkway with her son, who appeared to be about four years old. He was not the happiest camper being whisked in such a hurried fashion. All of a sudden he flung himself to the ground, and started to throw a temper tantrum. The hurried mom then did an amazing thing. She did not try to argue with the little guy, she did not yell at him or try to drag him along. Rather, without a moment's hesitation, she dropped to her knees, put her arms around the boy, and hugged him very closely. Even though she was right in the middle of the walkway, with people hurrying around them, she gave her full attention to her disgruntled child.

This was an unusual sight. However, in about 30 seconds, they both stood up. The boy took his mother's hand and they continued their journey at an even faster pace than before. There was no sign of struggle or sense that the child resented being dragged along.

What this mother had done was give up her goal-directed behavior for a brief moment, to meet the energy of her child. In doing so, she diverted a power struggle. No temper tantrum, no raising of a voice, no fighting. Instead there were a few moments of intimate tenderness, and right in the middle of a busy airport. Instead of trying to control him, she calmed his energy down and moved on even more efficiently than they were moving before the mini-rebellion had started.

When this story was finished, James said, "Wow. You are right. My style gets in the way of intimate moments of sharing. And I hurt my wife in the process. Why couldn't I just have gone with her idea for just a minute before I shut her down? Why couldn't I turn my one-track mind off, like that mother did, so I could see that just because we were going on a ski trip didn't mean we couldn't try something else as well? I really blew it, I missed an opportunity to share her enthusiasm. I missed an opportunity for intimacy."

The psychologist told James that yes, he had missed that moment. But he could go home and share with Maggie what he had just become aware of during his counseling session. He could apologize for shutting her down with such harsh words and tone and could share his sadness about that loss.

This was a difficult scenario for James to imagine, as it would be out of character for him. However, the next time, it might be a little easier for James to be more flexible and less rigid. And, since Maggie would hear his apology and explanation, she might be more understanding of those lawyer attributes that cause him to unintentionally hurt her in that way.

Leave a nice message on your lawyer's voice mail. Send a bouquet of flowers to the office to show how much you appreciate him. Stick a love note in with her lunch or gym bag. Send a thank you to him via e-mail. Thank your lawyer for a small thing.

In Contempt of Court—Or Your Partner

John Gottman, Ph.D., psychology professor at the University of Washington and the founder and director of the Seattle Marital and Family Institute, has studied the habits of married couples. In his book, *Why Marriages Succeed or Fail...and How You Can Make Yours Last,* he identified four dynamics that have the potential to destroy a marriage if they continually exist in your communication. These dynamics are:

1. Criticism

2. Contempt

3. Defensiveness

4. Stonewalling

While we are all guilty of these at some time or another, if they are frequently used in a relationship, the relationship is likely to fail. Note that these four dynamics are also successful courtroom strategies. A trial lawyer can score points by criticizing a witness for the other side. A prosecutor can show contempt for a defendant on the stand proclaiming innocence. A divorce attorney can show defensiveness for her client, an abused wife. A contract attorney can stonewall during a negotiation.

> **It is important for you to understand that not only is your lawyer using these four dynamics, but that you may be as well—perhaps in a more subtle style. It is not uncommon to find that the partner of a lawyer might use a quiet voice in an argument, but be just as guilty of carrying a big stick!**

One couple who came into therapy was constantly arguing about the fact that the wife didn't screw the caps onto bottles tightly. However, rather than registering a complaint about the situation in a loving manner, the lawyer put her on the witness stand and basically assassinated her character:

"Did you get something out of the refrigerator? Did you open the new bottle of soda? I bet you didn't screw the cap back on!" If she would attempt to respond, he would get louder and louder. "You are totally incompetent and just too lazy to do things right. You can't even screw the damn lid on a bottle."

At this point, the couple is in big trouble. This is not a conversation about the chance of the soda going flat; he has hurt her very core and being. This is not only ineffective communication, it is hurtful and difficult to overcome.

Another couple who came into therapy demonstrated how contempt can harm a relationship:

A wife asks her husband if he can help her get the house ready for company the following night. Before he has a chance to respond, she said, "You are never here when I really need you." He replies that he will try to come home early if he can change a meeting he has with a client at happy hour. She then says, very quietly, "Do you really think you will be able to say no to your client?" He replies, "I will make an effort." She then smirks, as if to say, "Yeah, right," and says "Sure you will. Like you would blow off your client to help me." "I'll try to move any appointment I have to lunch time," he replies. "Oh great," she says. "What are you going to do now, start drinking at lunch, too?" "Forget it," he finally responds. "Get the house ready yourself. I will be at work."

There were several opportunities in this example where the wife could have backed off and would likely have had her needs met. Instead, she treated her husband with contempt. If she had only recognized how her words, tone, and body language affected their conversation, there would have been a much greater opportunity to repair the hurt and damage that had been done.

In each of the above scenarios, both couples were able to learn how to stop the criticism/contempt process that normally escalated to verbal character bashing. How did they accomplish this? It was really quite simple. Both partners must become aware of their behavior and make an effort to stop it.

The following are strategies for you to try when you are hit with these courtroom communication skills.

If your lawyer is using criticism or contempt:

Step 1: Take a deep breath, then exhale slowly.

Step 2: Do not become defensive or try to justify...and if you are guilty, own up to it. For example, "Honey, you are right, I did not clean the house today."

Step 3: Find something in the criticism with which you agree. You are eliminating an option for an argument to escalate by agreeing with the fact that this is indeed your lawyer's viewpoint.

Step 4: Try saying something like "You are right, you really feel that way"...or "You are right, you really do believe that."

Step 5: Remember your different styles; not every comment needs your response!

Step 6: Say to yourself... "(S)he really needed to say that... that does not mean I necessarily needed to hear it."

If your lawyer is defensive:

Step 1:   Know you are on the right track.

Step 2:   Keep quiet, because the worst thing you can do is dig too deep and then be right.

Step 3:   If you must discuss this particular issue, wait until another time to bring it up to break the pattern. And make sure you choose a time when your lawyer had a successful day at the office and is not any one of the following: tired, hungry, angry, preoccupied with a new case, or feeling sorry for him/her self. Good luck finding that time.

If your lawyer is stonewalling:

Step 1:   Recognize the stonewalling tactic. Watch for your lawyer to hinder the process, delay, stall, and procrastinate. Recognize the passive/aggressive style in which your lawyer will not say "no" to you directly. Instead, (s)he says "O.K., I'll do that later" and then later never comes.

Step 2:   Quit knocking your head into the stone wall. This is not a good time to resolve anything.

Step 3:   Using a baseball analogy...give it three attempts and then forget it, you have struck out.

Step 4:   Take a different approach or just do it yourself.

Remind yourself and your lawyer that you are a team, and on the same side.

The Last Word—On Getting the Last Word

A summation is a final argument or closing statement. It is the opportunity each side has to summarize what they believe the evidence has shown. The lawyer might comment on the evidence and put it in its most favorable light to support his or her position. Having the last word in any argument is a very strong tool. Who among us would not like to have the last word in every argument?

This concept becomes extremely important when living with a lawyer, because (s)he is always going to want to have the last word. Understanding, that the "final word" habit comes from years of law school and courtroom training, might help you better deal with this trait.

Overruled: A Case Study

Ruby is a very successful litigator who lives with Joel, a C.P.A. Their problems arise when they try to make decisions that affect both their lives. Joel and Ruby recently moved into a condo and prepared to redecorate. Joel said he had always wanted white as the main color of his house. Ruby proceeded to give example after example why white was impractical and not a good choice. She talked for 20 minutes about the shortcomings of white before she said, "Navy blue might be a better one." In the end, Ruby's oratory won the day. Joel gave up trying to get her to understand what was important to him, and to no one's surprise, the color scheme of Joel and Ruby's new house is navy.

Ruby can't understand why Joel seems to harbor such resentment toward her. After all, she "knows" that navy blue was an excellent choice.

So what's the issue here? Well, if Joel is going to let her have the last word, he needs to choose to not harbor anger about it. He also could let her know how he feels about what has happened. That won't change the situation, but he might feel better expressing himself.

It Takes Two to Tango

Your relationship with your lawyer is like a ballroom dance. Consider the saying, "It takes two to tango." The tango is a passionate dance, but if one person makes a wrong move, the dance is ruined and a dance partner can even get hurt. (Remember those high heels, ouch!) However, if both partners want to move to the same tune, if they are sensitive to where their partner is at all times, and if they want to dance together and have fun, they can do it. Life with a lawyer is indeed like a dance.

If your lawyer is somewhat awkward on the dance floor of communicating emotions, it is because awareness of emotions is not a lawyer's strong point. If you recall the lawyer personality, while lawyers are generally more intelligent than the general population, they are less in touch with their feelings. Allow for the awkwardness of the emotional dance and help your partner learn how this is done. If (s)he is dancing with his or her mind, and you are dancing with your heart, you are not going to be in sync. But you don't have to find a new dance partner. You might want to try his or her dance once in a while.

And remember, by nature of the lawyer personality, your lawyer, male or female, wants to lead. So let him or her lead and learn to follow so that the dance, at some point, becomes so graceful that you forget who is really leading. When you choose to follow, and are not just being pushed around, are you not really in the lead? You can fight to be the leader on the dance floor, or you can choose to be the follower. Help your dance be one filled with grace, harmony, and rhythm...the beat will go on!

Chapter 3

Good Lawyering vs. Poor Loving

*It is not what a lawyer tells me
I may do; but what
humanity, reason, and justice,
tell me I ought to do.*

—Edmund Burke

Chapter 3

Good Lawyering vs. Poor Loving

The characteristics that make a lawyer successful professionally are the same characteristics that can create problems in
their intimate and personal lives. But that obviously doesn't
mean that lawyers are not without strengths in relationships.
Lawyers are very capable of positive, healthy interactions at the
personal level. According to psychologist Dr. Stephen Feldman, the
lawyer's ability to think deeply and well, their conscientiousness,

---

The Lawyer's Appeal

A relationship with a lawyer can be a fulfilling and joyous one.
The author and her co-authors are living proof. Some of the characteristics of the lawyer personality can manifest themselves in positive ways. After all, being ambitious and articulate can certainly be
positives. And, a lawyer's personality traits often complement, not
compete with, those of his or her partner's. When asked what was
great about living with a lawyer, one wife said the following: "He is
bright, articulate, loves to problem-solve and is challenging."
When asked what the downside was, she responded "He is bright,
articulate, loves to problem-solve and is challenging."

---

sense of responsibility and accountability, and their basic belief that problems have solutions give them strengths crucial to relationship success. (Deborah Arron, "Lawyer Relationships," *ABA Journal,* October 1999.) There are aspects of the lawyer personality that, when used in a positive manner, can be beneficial to relationships.

The main problem, however, is that lawyers tend to not take the time to develop their emotional sides. They invest their energy into developing their professional selves, and practicing law is very demanding. Therefore, when there is a problem in the relationship, lawyers often do not acknowledge that it even exists. This is referred to as denial, and lawyers are very skilled at using this coping technique.

As a result of working with many lawyer couples, the following has been discovered: the most dreaded words a lawyer can hear from his or her spouse is "Let's talk!" When lawyers hear this statement, they automatically think "Oh no! What did I do now? Is this going to take up too much time? Am I going to be forced into one of those touchy-feely conversations?" This denial contributes to a lack of open communication, which is critical to a healthy relationship.

There are many articles that allude to a high divorce rate among lawyers as compared to other professions. It is our belief that the high divorce rate is due to:

- the lawyer personality, which includes this lack of development of emotions;
- long work hours;
- professional disillusionment;
- the unique stress of the legal profession;
- an unwillingness to seek professional help at the onset of the problems.

Susan Daicoff refers to the Tripartite Crisis composed of a decline in professionalism, low public opinion and lawyer distress. (Susan Daicoff, "Lawyer, Know Thyself," *American University Law Review,* Volume 46, June 1997.) The issues stated above and also repeatedly reported to the author in her clinical work with lawyers and their families, are the same ones that contribute to this professional crisis.

Female lawyers statistically have a particularly difficult time forming and maintaining intimate relationships. According to Deborah Arron, American Bar Association-sponsored studies report that almost a third of all women lawyers have never married as compared to eight percent of male lawyers; nearly half of all women lawyers are currently unmarried as compared to 15 percent of men. Compared to female physicians and college professors, women lawyers are less likely to be married, to have children or to remarry after a divorce, and are significantly more likely to become divorced. (Deborah Arron, "Lawyer Relationships," *ABA Journal,* October 1999.)

Who Lawyers Marry

Lawyers historically have married members of the helping professions, such as teachers, social workers, nurses, secretaries, counselors and stay-at-home moms. Regardless of the spouse's profession, lawyers instinctively gravitate to and ultimately choose partners who are Feeling, as opposed to Thinking, like themselves. They also tend to choose partners who are in professions that are not as time consuming as the law. This marital combination has been traditionally successful because they counterbalance each other's needs. However, problems arise when marital partners do not understand that each one of them is likely to have a unique and different view of the world. Problems will get worse when there is no respect for these differences.

Males have dominated the legal profession for centuries. Now, more women are attending law school, increasing the opportunity for males and females to meet during law school and while practicing law. Lawyers tend to exclusively socialize with each other more than many professions, providing the opportunity for fellow lawyers to meet, become involved in relationships, and fall in love. As a result, there are increasing numbers of lawyers marrying fellow lawyers.

The most successful dual-lawyer marriages occur when each marital partner practices in a completely different area of the law. For example, one practices in the private sector while the other is in the public sector. If they are both in the same arena; for example, the same law firm where they are competing with each other, the odds increase that they will be meeting in divorce court. This often occurs because both have the same strong lawyer attributes such as competitiveness, aggressiveness, high I.Q.s and low E.Q.s. They are generally great adversaries in the courtroom; it is in the intimacy of their private lives where these power struggles can be devastating.

If you are a lawyer who is married to another lawyer, it is recommended that you read this book together. You can have a successful lawyer marriage. But you must understand the dynamics of lawyer relationships. You need to recognize the personality traits that make for success in your professional lives but not in your personal lives. You must take responsibility for learning what is needed to achieve intimacy within your lawyer marriage. For success, it is crucial that you remind yourselves daily that the bedroom is not the courtroom, and your marriage is not about one partner winning and the other one losing.

The Healthy Relationship

Every relationship is unique. Your role and your partner's role in your relationship evolve out of your particular personalities and how they interact with each other. However, there are characteristics common to all healthy relationships. A healthy relationship includes:

- **Commitment:** Both partners have a long-term emotional investment in the relationship. At the first sign of a problem, they don't give up but work through difficulties to keep the relationship strong.

- **Unity:** Partners feel a sense of unity—"we"—while respecting each other's separateness and differences—the "I."

- **Respect:** Partners treat each other as equals and respect each other's contribution to the relationship. Each role is created equal. This means "never pulling rank." Partners provide each other with an environment that is free of abuse and harm.

- **Trust:** Partners earn each other's trust. Partners feel free to be themselves and share their thoughts and feelings openly and honestly.

- **Compromise:** Each partner does not have his or her own way at all times. Partners share control, take control and practice the art of yielding. As you enter onto an expressway where the traffic is moving at a high speed, there are signs that tell you to yield. This means you must be acutely aware of where the other drivers are and join them in a safe manner. It is the same in your relationship. By yielding we mean becoming aware of the other person and finding a safe way to join him or her as you travel the highway of life together. In our practice, we define yielding as actively meeting, not as giving up.

- **Acceptance:** Partners understand and accept their individual differences and let go of unrealistic expectations. They must truly accept their partner for the person (s)he is, not who (s)he wants the other to be. Partners don't attempt to control what the other thinks and feels.

- **Consideration:** Partners are kind to each other and think about how their behavior impacts the other person. Partners choose actions that strengthen their relationship.

- **Charity:** Partners give to each other, including support and encouragement. And forgive by letting go of anger and resentment.

- **Friendship:** Partners are each other's best friends who give the relationship priority. They are a primary, but not sole, source of nurturing and comfort.

- **Humor:** Partners know that laughter can be the best medicine. They laugh with, not at, each other. They know that life is short and they must take little things in stride.

The Good Merger

A corporate lawyer would define it in a different context, but our definition of a good merger is two individuals who have a solid sense of self and feel complete alone; who do not need each other but choose to share their lives together. In a good merger, there is interdependence. The term interdependence should not be confused with codependence. In codependent relationships, the partners cater to, and thereby encourage, each other's weaknesses. In interdependent relationships, they acknowledge each other's weaknesses but encourage each other's strengths. It might be helpful to think of interdependence in terms of collaboration. Collaboration is laboring together toward a common goal.

There is a great deal of literature about being codependent. Codependence is a psychological condition or a relationship in which a person is controlled or manipulated by another person who is affected with a pathological condition, such as an addiction to alcohol. The humorous definition of a codependent is that of one who, while on her deathbed, sees *everyone else's life* flash before her eyes. While people usually think of women as being codependent, many men are as well (it is just that women are more apt to buy those self-help books with codependent in the title). The least healthy relationships are those in which both parties are codependent, which results in the partners blaming each other for their own behavior and actions.

It is not uncommon for people in relationships with lawyers to be codependent. One reason is that lawyers often seem so confident in themselves and so firm in their answers. As a result, their partners back off and become enablers to the harmful behavior. Another reason is that lawyers go on the offensive, and the partner will often back down rather than risk getting into an argument.

In codependency, the partners cater to and encourage each other's faults and weaknesses. In interdependency, the partners do not encourage harmful behaviors, yet they acknowledge each other's limitations and learn to work with or around them. The partners appreciate each other's different and unique ways of being and behaving, and incorporate each other's gifts into themselves. As a consequence, they become more whole as individuals while still remaining connected.

The Lawyer and Intimacy

A lawyer once told his therapist that he needed a blood transfusion or something similar in order to understand what this "intimacy stuff" is all about! Often lawyers just don't get it. Intimacy is the emotional connection vital to a healthy relationship. Being emotionally close and supportive to others just does not come naturally. In Chapter 1, it was discussed how the Meyers-Briggs Personality Indicator categorizes people as Thinking and Feeling.

It is not uncommon to find the Thinking lawyer choosing a partner who is predominantly a Feeling type. This is not necessarily a problem, because research suggests this combination can make for a good team on a long-term basis. However, it can present difficulties if you do not understand that your partner is experiencing the world very differently; particularly if you, the Feeling partner, are seeking intimacy and emotional support from your Thinking lawyer.

Your lawyer might not even understand what emotional support is. This is true for both male and female lawyers. Female lawyers are less nurturing than the general population of women. So if you have a relationship with a female lawyer, do not expect that because she is female, she is going to be a "warm and fuzzy" kind of person. Regardless if the lawyer in your life is male or female, (s)he will require you to cut him or her some slack when it comes to relating at the feeling level.

Friction will occur in a relationship with your lawyer if you operate under the assumption that (s)he should know what you need, feel, and want. Unhappiness then results when your lawyer does not respond in the expected manner. After all, if (s)he loved you, he would automatically know what you want without you having to ask. Right? If you have to ask, it doesn't count because you had to ask. Right? Boy, can this dynamic render your lawyer feeling like he is "damned if he does and damned if he doesn't." Lawyers are smart, but they are not mind readers. Ask your lawyer directly for what you want.

The opposite dynamic can be just as destructive: that of your lawyer automatically believing (s)he knows what you need, feel, or want. In law school, lawyers are trained to think and speak for others. Thus, your lawyer might consciously or subconsciously, not only think, but also speak for you. This type of lawyer acts as if the other person is an appendage, and assumes that (s)he knows what the person wants. If your lawyer does this, you might be left feeling unappreciated and frustrated. On the other hand, there are those partners, (especially in long-term relationships with their lawyers), who choose to not let this behavior affect them negatively. Some partners empower their lawyers to think and speak for them. This could occur because the lawyer habitually takes over, is used to being in control, or just assumes (s)he knows best. If you do not resent your lawyer doing this, then it may not be a problem for you. However, if you do, then you need to learn how to empower yourself.

What is most important is that you recognize which of these dynamics apply to you, know if you are happy or unhappy with them, and always be discovering ways to take care of yourself.

The Jury is Still Out

Sarah is an excellent trial attorney in the District Attorney's office. She has all of the personality dynamics that help her win cases. She is bright, tough, competitive, articulate, driven, ambitious, highly skilled at arguing and unemotional in the courtroom. Unfortunately, she is also completely unaware of how these same dynamics are not attractive in a social environment. She is married to Ben, a self-employed contractor who builds upscale homes. When the couple is out to dinner with Ben's partner, who is married to a teacher, Sarah dominates the conversation and dominates Ben. She decides what everyone should eat, where they should go for after dinner drinks and when it is time to go. At home, she gets annoyed with Ben when he buys her flowers, because she doesn't care much for flowers. She wants jewelry. She thinks he should know what she prefers. (She has never told him, however. Oh, she has hinted plenty of times. But what is he? Stupid? It is so obvious to her.) Ben keeps trying to figure out how to make her happy, but he can never seem to do enough. No matter what, it never seems enough. She is never happy.

The jury is still out on whether this marriage will get a life sentence.

Ways to Achieve Intimacy Within the Lawyer Marriage

- Be specific about what supportive behavior you require. Then ask directly for it. Don't hint or beat around the bush. Lawyers often don't get it when you are specific about what you want, so they aren't likely to get it when they have to guess what you mean. Hints are worthless!

- Ask for what you need. Do not wait for your lawyer to develop mental telepathy. Don't assume if "(s)he really loved you, (s)he would somehow automatically just know!" Remember, lawyers are very intelligent, but they are not psychic.

- There is a vulnerability that comes with bonding and intimacy. Lawyers are trained to put on a tough facade and to hide any vulnerability, so intimacy can go against their grain. You can encourage your lawyer to be more comfortable being vulnerable by providing a safe haven in which (s)he can practice.

- Put yourself in your lawyer's place and really make an effort to see his or her point of view. This adds empathy and sympathy to a relationship and makes it easier for you to not take the other person's behavior so negatively and personally.

- Be patient. Recognize that giving emotional support does not come naturally to most lawyers. Call attention to times when (s)he is emotionally supportive by saying "thank you." When you thank your lawyer, note the specific instance of emotional support, for example, "Thank you for listening to me vent about my job." Accentuate the positive and eliminate the negative!

- Share your lawyer's professional life to any degree with which you are both comfortable. Have your lawyer tell you stories of his or her day over dinner. Ask questions. Learn the lingo, and learn about the field of law so that you can maintain a sense of bonding. Attend seminars and functions when possible. Read literature published by the legal associations. Educate yourself so you are truly interested in the law, but do not try to become a colleague. Your loving support is more important than collegial support.

- Remind yourself often when and how you met. Reminisce together about those early times. This can be difficult for your lawyer, because the legal profession trains them to be "in their heads," and reminiscing involves being emotional, or "in their bodies." Reminiscing as a couple can help you re-ignite the flames in your marriage.

Chapter 4

Loving Your Lawyer Without Losing Yourself

The only reward of virtue, is virtue;
the only way to have a friend
is to be one.

—Ralph Waldo Emerson

Chapter 4

Loving Your Lawyer
Without Losing Yourself

You are the most important person in a relationship. No matter who your partner is, you are the one in charge of your personal destiny and happiness. Knowing that everything starts and ends with you is self-fulfilling, not selfish. Being selfish means being self-centered to the point of lacking sensitivity toward others. Being self-fulfilled means you are not needy and dependent on others—particularly a significant other. Being self-fulfilled means you are in control of your own decisions, thoughts, and feelings. Do not give that power away. Self-fulfillment does not mean a disregard for others. It means a high regard for yourself. As one lawyer's wife stated, "Once I realized that I am really the only one in charge of me, my marital life was happier. I was responsible for me and sensitive to him!"

The least healthy relationships are those in which each person has given power away to the other partner. How do you avoid this and achieve a balance of power within a partnership, particularly when one of the partners is a lawyer? There is no perfect relationship. However, you can learn how to attain a sense of wholeness and to reach inner peace and acceptance of yourself and your lawyer—flaws, lawyer personality traits, and all! By feeling good about yourself, your relationship will also feel good.

Three Roles Played While Living and Loving a Lawyer: Rescuer—Victim—Persecutor

These roles are not only played out in the drama of our court-rooms everyday, they are likely to appear in the drama of your daily life.

The roles are often quite obvious in a triad of three people. You might think of a situation in which three people you know readily take on these roles. This happens quite easily in the family unit. For example, the lawyer Dad may be the Persecutor by criticizing the child. The mother sees the child as the helpless Victim about to have his ego bruised, and she steps in to protect him, thus becoming the Rescuer.

You might also know three people who each manifest one of these roles most of the time. It could be just how you think of them: Sally, the Victim; Joe, the Persecutor; Jane, the Rescuer. This means they take on these roles as a predominant way of interacting with others in their world. However, even if a person has a tendency to take on one role more than another, everyone manifests all three at one time or another. It simply is a human dynamic.

Within this dynamic, it is possible for you to manifest all three roles, changing so quickly from one to the other that you do not even see it occur. You can go from Rescuer to Victim, and turn quickly into a Persecutor, in a matter of seconds!

Karpman Triangle

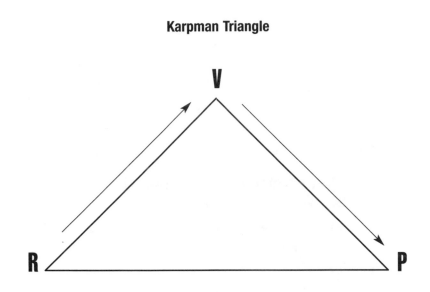

Here is how it works. If you are a chronic Rescuer, you are likely to become a Victim and feel sorry for yourself because you are always taking care of everyone else. And then when nobody, let alone the white knight riding in on his horse, rescues you, it is easy to get angry and strike out. Now, you have taken on the role of Persecutor.

Let's examine these three roles more closely:

Victims

In today's world, there are many people who want to blame everything on someone else, never wanting to take responsibility for their own fate. This naturally starts at a young age. Listen to children and you will hear them say "I didn't do it, she did!" "It is not my fault!" "He made me do it!" "Don't blame me!"

In our legal system, there is only one guilty party, and nobody wants to be it. As it is demonstrated in the drama triangle, it is relatively easy to become the Victim through one's own actions— like rescuing. For example, if you do not take care of yourself and are busy taking care of others, you are going to start feeling sorry for yourself. If you do not take the time you need for your own refueling and nurturing, you could easily be guilty of playing the role of the Victim.

Lawyers can also assume this role of Victim, causing those of us who live with them to want to rescue them and help them feel better. Susan Daicoff (see Chapter 1) reports a study by Satterfield, Monahan and Seligman. (1997) Pessimism was associated with high grades in law school while optimism was associated with low grades. The pessimism was so great that the negative beliefs were more pessimistic than those compared to persons with clinical depression. This pessimism was interpreted as "bad things are frequent and all my fault" and good things that happen are "by chance." If you are living with one of these bright, high-achieving yet pessimistic Victims, it's easy to see why you could want to rescue him or her to try to make life a little more pleasant.

Rescuers

Rescuers are peacemakers. They want everything to go well. They do not want to see anyone hurting, emotionally or physically. They often get in the middle of a Persecutor and a Victim. Unfortunately, Rescuers are often victimized by their own chronic need to rescue.

The lawyer personality tends to hook the rescuing role of the people who love them. Practicing the law is stressful and many lawyers have a short fuse. It is not uncommon, especially if you are a woman, to burden yourself by taking responsibility for the happiness of the lawyer in your life. For example, you may find yourself trying to make sure the children do all the right things and not fight or argue with each other so that the home front is a peaceful place for your gladiator of the court to relax. Or if your lawyer comes home in a bad mood after losing a big case, you may try to protect the children from the frustration that may get misfired at them. Moms are champion Rescuers, either rescuing children from Dad or saving Dad from the negative dynamics of the children.

Persecutors

Persecutors do just that: they persecute. Lawyers do this well. By nature, they are competitive, combative, aggressive, articulate and are quite good at criticism. Sometimes they are not even aware that this is their style. They can be Persecutors because it becomes a natural role within the study of law. Even when they are defensive, they can fall into this role. As previously indicated, Victims and Rescuers can also quickly become Persecutors in the drama triangle.

Do not judge these roles. They are not "good" or "bad." One is not any better than another. They exist in our everyday life. Although these roles are played out more clearly in the courtroom, they exist at many different levels in your life as well. Become aware of them and if you are in a role you do not like, take responsibility for changing it. Awareness is the first step to change.

The following is an example of this dynamic and how prevalent it is in our daily lives. You will see how Maggie, the mother, anticipates an uncomfortable situation between her teenage son, Alex and her lawyer spouse, Dan. By getting herself in the middle, she ends up going around the Triangle from Rescuer to Victim to Persecutor very quickly.

When in Hot Water, Call Your Lawyer: A Case Study

Teenage Alex habitually showers when he gets up in the morning and has begun to linger more and more in the shower as he has gotten older. Now, no matter how many bathrooms one has, most of us only have one water heater with a limited supply of the hot stuff. Almost on a daily basis, Maggie hears her husband Dan complain, before he even gets out of bed, that Alex is going to use up all of the hot water. The scene is set. Maggie tries to prevent her anticipated scene which is Dan will be angry and yell at Alex. Dan = Persecutor. Alex = Victim. Maggie = Rescuer.

Now at this point, Maggie starts jumping into the role of Rescuer to avoid hearing her husband let out a few chosen expletives as the hot water runs out during his shower. She jumps out of bed to rush Alex before Dan gets upset. "Alex, you are going to use up all the hot water. Hurry and get out of the shower." Alex becomes defensive or procrastinates and says "I'm almost through, I'll be out soon" and proceeds to remain in the shower longer. More requests from Maggie, more defensiveness from Alex. Nearly every morning has turned into an unpleasant scene between Maggie and Alex. Alex is not in the best mood to go to school, Dan is stressed out before he even leaves for his law practice, and Maggie is left with anxiety and frustration.

This is a common scene. Maggie got "hooked" into trying to make everyone happy and tried to keep Dan from getting upset. She started out to rescue, but got upset with Alex, herself. She ended up feeling sorry for herself (Victim) with nobody helping her feel better. Therefore, she ended up blaming Dan (she became a Persecutor) because he complained every morning. The cycle happened so fast, it was hard to understand exactly how it happened. After all, Maggie really meant well!

After many unpleasant mornings and stewing in her own hot water, Maggie realized she needed to change this routine. This was not about the hot water, it was about her jumping into the Rescuer role. She pulled herself out of this triangle. She suggested that Dan and Alex work out a shower schedule that allowed time for both to get ready and still have enough hot water. And it worked! Even if Dan complained, she did not react on autopilot without knowing the consequences of her rescuing syndrome.

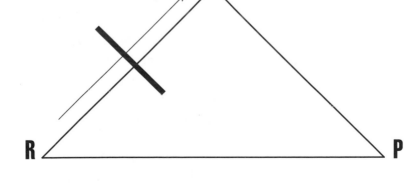

When your lawyer compliments you, be sure to say "Thank you...so nice of you to notice." Never discount a compliment.

Taking Responsibility

Responsibility means different things to different people. Most people agree that being responsible includes taking care of oneself and earning a living. Parents have the responsibility to raise their children to be responsible adults. It is an admirable goal to want your family to grow up and be able to meet their own needs and to be responsible citizens. Since there are no perfect parents, most adults have to finish the job for themselves.

Take responsibility for the unhappiness in your life just like Maggie did. Become aware, identify the problem, and make the changes that you need to make in order to feel better. Talk to yourself. Nurture yourself. If you start to feel like a victim, choose another route. Do something just for you. Do not sit around and wait for the knight in shining armor to come along and pull you out of the hot water.

Body vs. Mind

In order to take responsibility for changing yourself, you must first become aware. Awareness is the first step and the key to all change. It is important to know the thoughts in your mind. Also important, but perhaps not as easy, is to know what messages your gut feelings are telling you. The body is your resource for self-care. If you know yourself, you will realize you have a choice about how you are going to react to a situation. This way of responding to the world around you helps you feel more in control. Become more aware of both thoughts and feelings and you will find yourself in less hot water.

After becoming aware of a feeling, it is important to trust that the feeling is valid. Remember, feelings do not have to make sense, they just are! Most people trust their sense of "knowing" when thinking rationally. It is more difficult to get that same sense of confidence into our heart and soul where we feel, rather than think. Many lawyers, as well as their spouses, have expressed "I know it up here," pointing to the head, "but I cannot feel it in here," pointing to the heart.

It is hard to trust your own gut as valid and O.K., especially when you are living with one of those rational, lawyer creatures. You crave outside validity, then you will know you are O.K. However, keep in mind that lawyers have the most difficulty giving any credibility to gut reactions.

Recall the discussion regarding lawyers as Thinking vs. Feeling? Most lawyers trust information generated from their intelligent minds, but discount information generated in their feeling bodies. They do not trust their gut reactions and do not understand what is called body wisdom. Lawyers are rational and logical. Since it is hard for lawyers to know this intuitive knowledge, it is nearly impossible for them to validate your feelings. Do not try to change the lawyer in your life. The lawyer personality, having been reinforced with law school training, is not likely to change much. Therefore, your key to happiness in your life is for you to take responsibility for your own happiness and change yourself instead.

This is not an easy thing to do, but it is possible. However, in order to grow in this process, you cannot allow yourself to be intimidated by your lawyer's opinions and thoughts.

Reverse the Decision: A Case Study

Victor and Laura are at the dinner table at his law firm's holiday party. Laura is seated between her husband and Mike, a new partner at the firm. Victor has told Laura what a great guy Mike is, and how fortunate they are to have wooed him away from another firm. Victor has a high opinion of this new lawyer. When Mike tells a sexually risqué joke and winks at Laura, she has an uncomfortable gut reaction. She has an intuitive negative sense about this man right away. However, the others laugh loudly so she smiles as well. Mike then makes more comments that Laura thinks are inappropriate and her "gut" sense of him is "Maybe he is a great lawyer, but he is not much of a man!" However, since everyone laughs, it seems that everyone disagrees with her interpretation. Her self-doubt and anxiety increase, and she begins to doubt her own "guts." She must be wrong. As her anxiety increases, the lawyer intimidation factor also increases. It is easy to see how this dynamic can occur. "After all," she thinks, "they are all lawyers, they are bright, and they must know what is right."

During the dinner, Laura feels even more uncomfortable when Mike leans very close when he talks to her and touches her hair as he admires it. "The lawyers work with him and like him," she tells herself, "So he must be O.K. I must be wrong to feel uncomfortable when he is probably just a friendly guy." After dinner, Laura asks her husband if he thought Mike was out of line. "Oh, that's just the way Mike is," Victor tells her. "He is harmless." Now she really doubts her discomfort.

*Later in the evening, Laura is waiting alone out front
for her husband to bring the car around when Mike slips up
to her. He asks her if she is unhappy in her marriage and
tells her he could make her happy, "if you know what I
mean." He tries to kiss her. Laura pushes him away and
tells him to bug off, relieved to see her husband is pulling
the car up at that moment.*

*Now she has proof she hadn't been off track. She now
realizes that even though the other lawyers hadn't con-
firmed her thoughts, it did not necessarily mean she was
wrong in her interpretation. And, she didn't need to assume
that since they were lawyers, they must know what they are
talking about. When Laura tells her husband what happened, he is immediately sorry for doubting her feelings.*

Laura was lucky in this case because Mike was such an
obvious jerk that he helped make it easy for her to get back in
touch with her trust. It is not always that easy, and therefore, one
has to practice trusting those "gut feelings." **Fact: The body
does not lie.**

Why do we lose trust in our gut reactions? If you have grown
up with a lawyer as a parent, trusting your gut might be even more
difficult. Lawyers are renowned for questioning your body truths.

Child: "I have to go to the bathroom!"
Lawyer Parent: "Are you sure? You just went a little while ago."

This is a reasonable response and not a bad courtroom strategy.

Child: "I'm really hungry, I am totally starving."
Lawyer Parent: "You cannot be that hungry; dinner time is two
hours away."

Child: "I really wish I could have that new giant TV for my room!"
Lawyer Parent: "That is way too big and expensive for you."

These are three examples of how a gut feeling or a desire is met with total denial. Our entire culture gives more credibility to thoughts than to feelings. It is just that lawyers do it more! We learn to trust only pain as the sole piece of valid body information. The responses above are not irrational, in fact that is the problem, they are rational. It is important to understand, however, that it is through this rational process that we become distrustful of our gut feeling knowledge—information that is real and true when it occurs.

It might not be convenient or even possible for the lawyer to respond in an understanding way that gives credibility to the feeling. But, it does not mean the feeling is invalid. You cannot expect validity of feelings from your lawyer, who is trained to keep feelings out of the law. No judge is going to instruct a jury to go into the jury room and "Trust your gut reactions to all of this testimony and make your decisions based on them." Of course not. Become aware and understand that it is very difficult for a lawyer to turn off that whole way of thinking and change just because they are in the bedroom instead of the courtroom.

In the above examples, the lawyer responses are not synonymous with terrible parenting. It is simply a lawyer-like style that does not particularly help others, especially children, feel validated. And this situation is not exclusive to fathers. Although the majority of women in the general population are more Feeling than Thinking, this is not the case for female lawyers. They, too, are more Thinking than Feeling, and are therefore more likely to respond to their children and spouses in a similar rational manner.

Growing Up With a Lawyer as Your Parent

Growing up with a lawyer as a parent can be a challenge. Lawyers have a style that can either help you create a strong sense of self out of the necessity to survive, or bruise your ego at times. Growing up in any family is not easy. There are no perfect parents regardless of profession. A favorite cartoon is that of the annual convention of Adult Children of Functional Families and there is a lone member in the audience. One could say that 75% of us grow up in dysfunctional families and the remaining 25% are unreported! It is only how severely dysfunctional your family is that makes the difference. Chances are good that your family is relatively healthy.

The authors asked many children and adult children of lawyers the following question: "So what is it like growing up with a lawyer for your parent?"

Here are some of their comments:

- I was the only kid in junior high who turned in her homework on yellow legal paper.

- It was really great when I got my first speeding ticket!

- My dad was a lawyer and it was great compared to my mom, who was an emotional roller coaster. Although I never got a simple "yes" or "no" when asking my dad anything, I could count on him being rational.

- I learned to never ask for advice unless I was prepared to hear a long, very long soliloquy.

- Both of my parents are lawyers. They fight a lot. My mom usually is the one to make up first.

- It means never getting a quick, short answer to anything. If you ask a question, you get much more information than you ever need. After the first few minutes, you get the point and after awhile, you feel like you must be stupid or something. Either that or you just get confused again by too much answer. Sometimes you forget what you even asked!

- The best thing: every Wednesday was macaroni and cheese night in front of the TV when my Dad had night court.

- Conversations with my father were always more than I bargained for. If you ask a simple question, never expect a simple answer.

- You can always count on an explanation along with citations, especially in an e-mail!

- My mommy argues a lot. My daddy says she is supposed to. That is what she gets paid for. She is a lawyer.

Achieving and maintaining a state of well-being is no easy task in relationships with lawyers. The legal mind's rational explanation of your irrational feelings can be very intimidating. Feelings do not make sense, they just are. Not allowing the Thinking lawyer to dismiss the value of your intuitive body information is not easy, but it is a valuable dynamic that helps you keep from losing your "self" in the relationship. It takes awareness and practice, but it is well worth the results of feeling good about yourself and not depending on approval or affirmation from that legal mind.

Thus, if you are a Feeling person, you should recognize how difficult it is to trust your own gut sense of knowledge and your body truths when confronted with these lawyer-like reasonable responses all of the time. Trusting your gut takes awareness and practice. Trusting yourself is empowering. When this process occurs, then the demand that your lawyer partner change who (s)he is, just so you can be O.K., ceases to exist. And, both you and your lawyer can be much happier in your relationship.

The Lawyer's Appeal

Your lawyer's tendency to look at things rationally, as a Thinker, can have its positive effects on your relationship. A Feeler has a tendency to overreact and let emotions cloud judgment at times and the logical viewpoint of the lawyer can be a welcome counterbalance.

Helene's husband calls to tell her the law firm for which he works might merge with another larger one. She immediately envisions her husband laid off, having to find a new job. Upset, she begins drilling him with questions: "What will happen to your benefits?" "Will we have to dip into our retirement account? What about the vacation we were planning?" Her husband suggests she take a deep breath and calm down. The merger is only in the early discussion phase, and he has been told that he will have even more opportunities in the new firm if it goes through. Besides, he tells her, if it doesn't work out he will find new work and they could think about moving to the ocean as she always wanted. His rational thinking helps put the situation into perspective.

Becoming Aware of Your Body Signals

There is a strong connection between the body and the mind. How this affects your stress level is addressed in Chapter 5. It is essential that you become aware of your body's signals to know what you are feeling, to trust the validity of the signals, and to find healthy ways to express the energy. This helps to give you a sense of yourself so you do not lose who you are.

For purposes of awareness, think of your whole body as a large pot of water on the stove. It cannot boil instantly. There is a process in which the water goes from cool (your body in a calm state) to the boiling point (your body in a fit of rage.) If you watch water in a pot on the stove, the first thing that occurs is the formation of a tiny bubble on the bottom of the pan. Then, several tiny bubbles appear. The next phase has the bubbles rising and creating a rolling motion known as simmer. The final step is the water reaching the boiling point. And, if the pot is too full and not carefully monitored, it does in fact, boil over.

If a recipe says, "Do not boil," you pay attention and you stop the process before the water gets to that point. If you don't want to boil, then you must watch your own "pot" and pay attention. Most of us are aware when we are in boil, but few of us are aware of the first little bubble that forms on the bottom of the pan. This bubble is often a feeling in the pit of your stomach. The energy of anxiety literally rises in the body. The voice even goes up in pitch as we become more and more upset. The heart rate increases, the face flushes, and our palms can even become sweaty.

Some of you may be walking around all the time in the simmer stage. Therefore, it requires less heat for you to reach the boiling point. Whether it is anger, sadness, or fear that you are simmering in your pot, not being aware of the first little bubble can cause you to feel out of control when you begin to boil over.

A Side Bar on Feelings

The basic human emotions are fear, anger, joy, and sadness. Stay only with these four when you practice becoming more aware of gut feelings. It is easier to identify what you are feeling and find the appropriate expression to release the feelings.

Pay attention to the first small rumblings generally located in your abdomen or chest. At the same time, notice your breathing. When the bubbles are forming in your pot (your body) the breath often is interrupted. It will be very shallow or completely suspended for a moment.

This is the survival hormone, adrenaline, getting ready to pump in order for the body to "fight or flight." Somehow, it appears as though your survival is at stake. It is! Your life may not be threatened, but your ego is!

In a relationship with a lawyer, you must learn how to strengthen your own ego. Lawyers have enough trouble with their own egos, so they cannot be responsible for feeding yours. Give up trying to get help strengthening your ego from the lawyer in your life.

"The first thing we do, let's kill all the lawyers."
—William Shakespeare

Coping With Anger

Anger is one of the four basic human emotions. A book about being successful at living with a lawyer definitely needs to mention coping with anger. Now, what could it be about a lawyer that would provide such a wonderful opportunity to identify anger and find healthy ways to express it? Could it be any number of their attributes: their competitiveness, especially if it is with you? Their perfectionism, especially if they demand it of you? Or being that rational lawyer when you need emotional support? Pick any number of the lawyer attributes and at some time in your relationship, it is likely that you became angry that your lawyer was just not who you wanted him or her to be. And when things are not the way we would like for them to be, anger is the normal, and we might add, healthy response.

It is not being angry that causes problems; it is staying angry that is damaging. Knowing that your lawyer will give you plenty of opportunities to be angry, the following guidelines will help you to cope.

Awareness is the key to all change. Becoming aware of that first "bubble" or low-level frustration or irritation is the first step in managing your anger in any relationship you have. Identify it and then own it. It is O.K., even healthy, to feel anger.

Normal emotional response to not getting things your way is anger. Trust your anger as a natural emotional energy and take responsibility for it. Understand that it is normal to have anger. You are not weak or crazy when you experience this feeling.

Grow as a person with your experiences of anger. Use your anger as an opportunity to grow in your understanding of yourself, your family, your history, and your life. What purpose is the anger serving in your life at this time?

Express your anger in healthy ways. This expression can be done verbally or nonverbally, through conversations or through physical activity as a stress reliever. Did you know that jogging is a vertical temper tantrum? That's right. If you were to lie down on your back and go through the movements of jogging, it would look like a two-year-old throwing a royal tantrum.

Respond vs. React. You can choose to respond from a variety of options available to you as opposed to operating on automatic pilot. Remember! Before you have spoken, you are in control of the words. After you have spoken, your words gain the power.

Just a Joke

A doctor told her patient that his test results indicated that he had a rare disease and had only six months to live.

"Isn't there anything I can do?" pleaded the patient.

"Marry a lawyer," the doctor advised. "It will be the longest six months of your life."

From a Lawyer's Perspective

—An anononymous letter to the author

The following are some thoughts on the "pulls" in the lawyer's life, each of which demands primacy, if not exclusivity. These are exaggerated to make the point.

1. The clients. They entrust you with the most important of their affairs, on a strictly confidential basis, in the context of a unique professional relationship that often is packed with emotion. They frequently expect your undivided attention, to the exclusion of your other clients who, of course, also expect your undivided attention. After all, the event that led them to hire a lawyer in the first place, no matter how common or mundane in the legal world, is something that may have happened to them for the first time and has become all consuming. Clients don't care about the other demands on your time and energy—they have a serious problem and you have to deal with it.

2. The courts, if you are a litigator. Every judge has to move his own docket. Most are considerate of the commitments lawyers have in other courts and jurisdictions, but the fact of the matter is that every morning you open your mail there is a chance you will find an order requiring you to be someplace that conflicts with an order directing you to be someplace else, or requiring you to devote attention to something that will take time away from something else that just won't wait. The point is, you rarely control your own life.

3. Other lawyers. In my city in Ohio, at least, most lawyers are still courteous to one another, but that is not true in other cities and states. Regardless of the locale, lawyers are under tremendous pressure from the clients to win. It's a very competitive business and every day involves a fight. Your upbringing and human nature tell you to be a conciliator, but the world you live in demands a jerk—you resist that and it's an everyday stress, but you have to pay constant and immediate attention to what the opposition is doing.

4. The Code of Professional Responsibility. In Ohio, it's composed of broad statements of concepts (Canons), aspirational missives (ethical considerations) and rules (Disciplinary Rules). The Code governs the conduct of all lawyers and your right/license to practice is dependent on compliance. The Code and the folks who enforce it (The Supreme Court) are mindful of the difficulties of the practice, but do not consider stress and difficulty to be an excuse for failure to comply with the Code's standards. In that respect, the Code is fairly unequivocal and unforgiving. But the precepts of the Code not only clash occasionally with the demands of the client, there are contradictions and tensions within the Code itself. For example, how do you reconcile the Disciplinary Rules' mandate that a lawyer "shall" maintain the confidences and secrets of a client with the equal mandate that a lawyer "shall" disclose every instance where a client has, even without the lawyer's present knowledge, lied or deceived a court or tribunal? Isn't that ratting out the client and exposing the client to criminal and civil sanctions? On top of all this, the Disciplinary Rules are viewed as the "minimum" standard of conduct we expect from lawyers.

5. **Your partners/solo office/small firm.** It's a business and it demands attention. If there's no paper in the copier, nobody cares if the reason is that you've been nearly destroyed in a four-week trial with very difficult clients, dishonest opposing counsel and an astonishingly stupid judge; they just want paper in the copier. Same with health insurance for the secretary, a parking space for the messenger, stamps for the mailroom, soft drinks in the break room, lights, phones, heat, etc., etc.

6. **Your children.** They're children—the world revolves around them. They don't have any idea what your world is like and you wouldn't want them to know.

7. **Your spouse. (See children, above).** They will never understand or appreciate what you do all day to earn a living. They are only mildly interested, and then mostly in how much money you bring home and how long you're going to bring it. After that, the focus is on how much time you can devote to the household chores and routines that have to be addressed on a daily basis. A catastrophe in your practice that turns your life into a living hell is important for only two reasons: a) will it affect the flow of cash into the household, and b) does it mean that I have to take the garbage out by myself?

Where, in all this, is time for the lawyer to be irresponsible, spontaneous, curious, human? Where did the lawyer's life go and does anybody care? This is why lawyers drink.

—A Stressed Lawyer

Chapter 5

Stress Happens: To Both You and Your Lawyer

Give me your tired, your poor,
your huddled masses
yearning to breathe free.

—Emma Lazarus, "The New Colossus"

Chapter 5

Stress Happens: To Both You and Your Lawyer

Warning: Being a lawyer can be harmful to your health. The surgeon general might not issue a warning on the law school application, but the risk is there. Lawyers are a high-risk population for stress-related health problems, including heart attacks, depression, substance abuse, gastrointestinal disorders, and even cancer. And, lawyers are not the only victims of law-related stress. If you live with a lawyer, you also face unique stressors as well. While there is literature geared toward lawyers and their stress, little attention is paid to the effects of lawyers' stress on their relationships and on their significant others. While this chapter explores how and why lawyers are stressed, it does not overlook the stress you face when living with your lawyer.

An attorney was overheard saying, "I do not suffer from stress-related illnesses. I'm simply a carrier of them!" While this attorney was kidding, it conveyed an element of truth. You may know too well what this statement means. A denial of a lawyer's stress means wives, children, secretaries, legal aids, paralegals, interns and even other attorneys catch what (s)he is passing on.

Whether a lawyer's area of specialization is criminal law or tax law, environmental law or personal injury law; whether they work in a public or private setting; their breeding predisposes a certain way of thinking, feeling and behaving. These patterns often result in situations that have been described throughout this book—a thriving professional life combined with an unhappy personal and intimate life. Also, the practice of law is the most demanding of the professions. Lawyers daily are pulled in a variety of directions and each is demanded to be given primacy.

There is a public distrust of the legal system, and there is also a growing dissatisfaction within the profession among lawyers themselves. Walt Bachman calls the practice of law a high-risk profession. There is a disproportionately high incidence of depression among lawyers. Lawyers also are more likely to be addicted to alcohol and other drugs. Lawyers are notorious workaholics. There is a high rate of divorce among lawyers. And, stress-related health conditions such as heart attacks, ulcers, and high blood pressure also are more common in the law profession than most other fields. (Walt Bachman, *Law v. Life: What Lawyers Are Afraid to Say About the Legal Profession*, 1995, Four Directions Press, Rhinebeck, NY) All of these factors take their toll on a relationship.

Relationships aren't easy. The pressures of the field of law and the unique personality of the lawyer can make the relationship dynamics even more challenging.

What is Stress?

One definition of stress: An individual's perceived inability to cope. The key word in this definition is the word "perceived." What stresses one person might not stress another. People in general, and lawyers in particular, like to know they have choices and control over their lives. If this sense of security is threatened by feeling overwhelmed and not in control, coupled with a fear of not being able to handle it all, the result is stress.

Physical Signs of Stress

- Headaches
- Insomnia
- Chest pains
- Fatigue
- Anxiety
- Heartburn
- Gastrointestinal disorders
- Difficulty swallowing
- Asthma
- Skin disorders
- Cold sweats
- Neck pain
- Backaches

Psychological Signs of Stress

When a lawyer is stressed, psychological dynamics emerge as well. The lawyer personality is particularly vulnerable to the following:

Defensiveness: Defensiveness reflects the unrealistic expectations that a lawyer should not show weakness or stress. The phrase, "Never let them see you sweat!" could be a lawyer's motto. Defensiveness can also manifest itself as self-blame and self-criticism.

Depression: Underlying depression is a feeling of anger or sadness. Lawyers, who want to be omnipotent, often feel anger and a sense of loss when they cannot control every aspect of their lives.

Disorganization: Stress preoccupies and diminishes concentration. As a result, disorganization can show up as sloppiness, absent-mindedness, and lapses in judgment; for example, missing a court date or not filing a brief in a timely manner.

Defiance: Lawyers, who are trained to be combative, tend to fight back when they feel stressed—even when there is no actual focus for their defiance. They might challenge authority like the judge in a trial, or become overly argumentative.

Dependency: Many lawyers regress while under stress. They would love to be saved and to be taken care of, but rarely will they admit this fantasy to others, or even to themselves. Often they add to their stress by denying or feeling guilty about this need.

Decision-Making Difficulties: Feeling stressed usually means feeling a lack of control, choice, or preparation in a situation. Making decisions, even minor ones, under such conditions can be very difficult. Deciding what to wear to court becomes overwhelming.

What causes stress?

Belief System: Rational vs. Irrational

Although lawyers are more thinking than feeling, and they are generally reasonable and prudent, it does not mean they never have irrational thoughts like everyone else. The following model and diagram will help in your understanding of how these irrational beliefs create a lot of stress for lawyers and their loved ones.

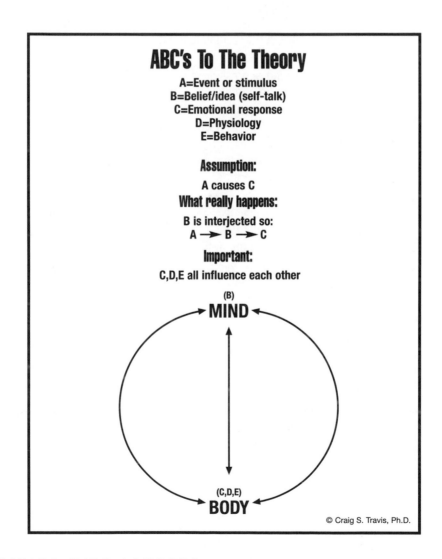

ABC's To The Theory

A=Event or stimulus
B=Belief/idea (self-talk)
C=Emotional response
D=Physiology
E=Behavior

Assumption:

A causes C

What really happens:

B is interjected so:
A → B → C

Important:

C,D,E all influence each other

(B)
MIND

(C,D,E)
BODY

© Craig S. Travis, Ph.D.

The assumption is that A causes C, or the event (or stimulus) directly causes the emotional response. For example, your lawyer is very late coming home and you get angry. You believe that his lateness caused your anger. However, what really happens is that A leads to B which is what really causes C. Returning to our example, your lawyer being late does not cause the anger. Rather, it is what you are telling yourself about that late behavior that causes an angry reaction, like "he does not care" or "he always put his work before the family." As a result of anger, the body becomes tense, adrenaline flows (D, body response) and then one might do something like yell, pout, or whatever you do when angry, which is the resulting behavior (E).

Your stress is not created by situations or events, but rather by what you tell yourself about that event. And what you tell yourself is generally irrational. An example of irrational thinking is you are upset when you learn that another attorney's wife, whom you dislike, does not like you either. You want to be liked by everyone, even by people you do not like. Now, how rational is that?

Let's look at how this model is relevant to interactions with your lawyer.

Presumed Guilty: A Case Study

Larry, a lawyer, and his date Johanna are attending a legal function. Johanna offers her opinion on a recent trial that received a lot of media attention. She sees Larry raise his eyebrows as she is speaking. Raised eyebrows = A, the stimulus. Johanna immediately tells herself that she has embarrassed Larry and is stupid for trying to say something about the law with a bunch of lawyers. This is B—her negative self-talk. She gets very upset that she has spoken up. Getting upset is C—her emotional response. Her face turns bright red and her stomach gets tight which is D—body response. She excuses herself and goes to the ladies room, where she hides out until the cocktail hour is over which is E—Johanna's behavior.

This all happened very quickly. We will return to this scenario later. However, keep in mind that the trigger in this situation was the raised eyebrow.

There are two kinds of beliefs:

1. Irrational beliefs, which when examined and studied carefully, do not make sense. For example, your belief that everyone should like you. These kinds of thoughts on a constant basis can lead to low self-esteem and high stress levels.

2. Rational beliefs, which when examined and studied carefully, do make sense. For example, your realization that all people are different and have different ideas and therefore, the whole world is not necessarily going to like you. Now, it would be nice if they did, and the world might even be a better place in which to live. But it is just not realistic. How could everyone like you? No matter how great you may be, there will be someone out there, because of who *they* are and *their belief* system, who simply will not like you. Believing and accepting that you are still a good person, in spite of the fact that someone does not like you, is what helps to reduce your stressful anxiety and increase your self-esteem.

To take responsibility for your own self-esteem, learn to identify the following irrational beliefs:

- **Absolutist thinking:** the use of the words never and always. For example, you might say, "I will never be able to get over this." or "This always happens to me..."

- **Using musts and shoulds:** the belief that someone or something must or should happen a particular way all of the time. For example, the belief that your lawyer should be available for all of the children's soccer games, even when involved in a big trial; the belief that your lawyer should get excited about the exact same things that you do, and express it the same way; and the belief that your lawyer should be ready to listen when you are finally ready to talk. Or vise versa.

- **Awfulizing:** using negative self-talk. For example, playing "ain't it awful"—taking a scenario to its catastrophic end: "It is terrible the way the senior partners treat John. He will never get ahead and make senior partner and we will never be able to move into a bigger house and we won't have any retirement income and the kids will have to put us in a state home! (Adapted from Ellis, Albert, *Reason and Emotion in Psychotherapy: Revised and Updated.* 1994. Carol Publishing Group.)

Let's revisit Larry and Johanna at the legal function. Johanna has been silent since her perceived faux pas. Johanna and Larry are now seated at dinner with a different group, and the conversation turns again to the recent trial. "Johanna, tell everyone what you said about the case before. That was really on target. I hadn't thought about it quite that way," Larry says. Johanna realizes that when Larry had raised his eyebrows he was expressing his pleasure with her insight. He was proud of her. A long way from being embarrassed. She had become a victim of her own irrational thinking.

Now, in this example, Johanna was fortunate because Larry helped set her straight before she allowed herself to get really depressed. If she had read this book, Johanna herself might have figured out her interpretation of Larry's raised eyebrows just might not be the right one. Definitely, her assumption is not the only one. Raised eyebrows could be interpreted any number of ways. With a little self-talk, she could have returned from hiding out in the bathroom, having boosted her own ego.

The scenario with Larry and Johanna is a good example of how this dynamic can cause unnecessary stress in your life. In our counseling with lawyers and their loved ones, we remind them that they will fall into this irrational belief trap. We all do. **The key is to know what you are thinking, take responsibility for it, and choose not to stay in the sad, mad, bad, gloomy trap too long!**

Stress and Fatigue

What happens when you fall in these traps and don't manage stress effectively? One of the results is fatigue. There are three types of fatigue: physiological, pathological, and psychological.

Physiological fatigue is a result of chemical reactions in healthy people that leave the muscles exhausted. Lack of sleep, loud noise, poor working environment, and extreme temperatures are examples of this kind of fatigue.

Pathological fatigue is severe chronic tiredness. It can be a sign of an illness or disease, including diabetes, hypertension, anemia, a heart defect, a sleep disorder, flu, or Lyme disease. It could be chronic fatigue syndrome or it could be just plain old tired!

Psychological fatigue, also called nervous fatigue, is caused by mental and emotional factors. It might be triggered by frustration, difficult decisions that need to be made, conflicts, delays, and even boredom. Studies have demonstrated that a majority of fatigue is psychological, caused by emotions.

Having a variety of emotions is normal. Everyone feels anger, anxiety, guilt, sadness, and frustration at times. Emotions are experienced in the body and produce a physical reaction, including muscle tension. If these emotions are not expressed in a healthy way, the emotional energy that remains in the body depletes physical energy and results in fatigue. The body becomes a holding tank for emotions. Often, one learns in childhood to "hold back, hold in, hold out and hold up."

How many times have you heard a parent say, "Anger doesn't solve anything." True, anger doesn't solve a problem, but it is the normal, natural reaction when something is not going the way you want it to in your life. It is how you cope with anger, not the anger, which can be healthy or harmful.

Anger, fear, and rage send adrenaline through the body, affecting breathing, and causing the heart to beat more rapidly. Adrenaline is the natural survival hormone that prepares the body for the "fight or flight" response. After adrenaline stops pumping through the body, it is normal to feel tired. However, some people remain on adrenaline overload, which can wear on the body. Others have sensitivity to the body's adrenaline, causing a chronic state of anxiety and possibly panic attacks.

A healthy dose of adrenaline can really be a great vehicle for a lawyer creating a good legal argument. However, if emotions are not identified and expressed, they remain in the body and become a vehicle for creating a state of depression. Depression is energy being pressed down and held within. Depression can be a result of overwhelming stress, a pessimistic personality, genetic predisposition, and hormonal imbalances such as serotonin levels.

The Stress Lawyers Face

From the beginning of law school and forward into the field of law, lawyers face many unique factors that contribute to their stress.

The "Dream" of Being a Lawyer

Many law students enter law school with an idealistic view of the legal profession. By the time they graduate, reality has started to sink in. Why do people choose to enter law school in the first place? An interest in the subject matter, a desire for training in a profession, and a desire for intellectual stimulation topped the list of student answers. However, there also is a hidden agenda for many that being a lawyer means earning a high salary and having power.

The Burden of Law School

The author, speaking to law students at The Ohio State University College of Law, asked students what caused them the most stress. The majority quickly responded that it was the financial burden of attending law school. Many students had enormous student loans and faced pressure to get high paying positions once they graduated in order not to have debt for a lifetime. Many law students end up choosing jobs in different areas of the legal profession than they had planned because they cannot "afford" to take the job they had hoped for and feel compelled to accept the highest bid.

Many lawyers today enter the profession with the expectations of their law career bringing them prestige and sense of well-being. Supreme Court Justice Rehnquist stated that many lawyers in the profession are working harder, making more money—and enjoying life less. Why is there such career dissatisfaction among lawyers today? Many lawyers want to save the world, to protect justice, and have other worthy goals, but end up spending more time pushing paper in the library than in the courtroom.

One reason for this dissatisfaction is that lawyers can end up practicing in an area of law that does not match their personality. Law schools do not provide specialization and residencies requiring students to soul search which specialty suits them best. Rather, a regular job search process dictates the nature of the law practiced. The type of law a lawyer ends up practicing might be what a practice or agency needs when the person is hired. Often lawyers become experts in their area of practice by default, rather than by a carefully thought out decision-making process.

Often, lawyers pour their heart and soul into their workplace, hoping to become partner. But, hard work and long hours no longer guarantee partnership. Lawyers' hopes might be dashed if they don't make partner by a certain age. Nowadays, firms are bought, sold, and merged, and lawyers are victims of reorganization and downsizing.

Presumed Guilty: A Case Study

It is not only the lawyer who might be disillusioned; significant others are also affected.

Greg is married to Jennifer. When Jennifer was in law school, she had planned to become a civil rights lawyer, and champion causes for people in need. However, when she graduated law school, she was hired by a large corporation. As she made more and more money and moved up the corporate ladder, she became more comfortable with the role and rejected her earlier career goals of civil rights law. Greg was unhappy that Jennifer had chosen a different career path than she had anticipated and felt she had sold out. He sat in judgment of her decision and found himself being angry with her over every little thing. She was a good lawyer and he did not criticize her legal skills. However, he began criticizing her domestic skills!

Greg was miserable and realized he needed to deal constructively with his anger with Jennifer for choosing a different path than they both expected. After all, she was happy making more money and practicing in a different area of law. With a little coaching, he began to change his negative thought pattern.

First, he listed all of the positive things his wife was doing in her existing position. His list included donating to charity, taking on several pro bono civil rights cases, winning a lawsuit for an elderly woman who had been victimized by the system, and mentoring young people. This list helped him realize that although his wife had chosen a different career path, she still was making a valuable contribution to the community. Second, he reflected on the fact that his wife enjoyed her job. He realized that she might not have been so happy as a civil rights lawyer. Greg had to confront his own unhappiness and work through his grief of what he perceived he had lost. Once he realized how he was making himself so miserable, he changed and began to really appreciate Jennifer for who she is, as a person, and how she chooses to practice law.

Client Pressure

Clients can be very demanding, unappreciative and dissatisfied with the results of their cases. Remember, when lawyers fight for their clients in court, there is most often only one winner. So somebody loses. Some lawyers today are choosing to practice mediation for this very reason. However, the majority is still in a win-lose battle every day. When sharing a losing result with an unhappy client who does not understand how the law works, a lawyer reported finding the following explanation helpful: "It is not always about what is fair, it is about what the law allows." Many clients may still want their day in court, nonetheless.

Lawyers often have to work with clients who are facing the most stressful and painful times in their lives. For example, criminal defense attorneys work with people who are facing prison or even a death sentence; prosecutors work with victims who have lost family members; personal injury attorneys work with people who have been injured; tax attorneys work with clients who are being audited, and divorce attorneys work with couples who are fighting each other for custody of their children. Some clients require intense emotional support, and remember, emotions do not make sense to most lawyers.

According to Walt Bachman, lawyers can be dealing with clients who are:

- Unyielding, unreasonable, and unable to see the other person's point of view;

- Fixated on the pursuit of money to the exclusion of other personal qualities or standards of decent conduct;

- Personally troubled, whether because they are in financial distress, suffering from alcoholism, dependent on other drugs, or mentally ill;

- Contentious to the extent of thirsting for a fight;

- Downright dishonest; and

- Incompetent, often seeking to explain away their own shortcomings by blaming others.

(Walt Bachman, *Law v. Life: What Lawyers Are Afraid to Say About the Legal Profession,* 1995, Four Directions Press, Rhinebeck, NY)

Certainly, not all clients fall into the above categories. There are many lawyers who really like their clients and even socialize with them. But since clients can have these qualities, the risk of the following stress for lawyers is ever present.

The Threat of Malpractice

We are a litigious society. People want to sue for every little injustice—good work for attorneys unless they are the ones being sued! However, there are suits brought against lawyers and this does create stress.

Given the nature of the law, when you go to court, someone generally loses. As a result, some clients are not happy with the results. Often they do want to blame someone. Therefore, the threat of a lawsuit against the lawyer is ever present.

Just a Joke

Q: What did the lawyer name his daughter?
A: Sue.

Occupational Hazards

Lawyers face many occupational hazards. These include long hours, especially in the private sector; lack of sleep; physical exhaustion; excessive worry; high anxiety; the possibility of violence, especially in the practice of domestic relations; and the almighty billable hour.

Being a lawyer can be a very demanding and time-consuming profession that leaves little time for family life. Many lawyers' careers are based on the number of billable hours they obtain, which can cause them to work endless hours. Most of us do not seem to have enough time for our significant others, children, and home as it is. Lawyers, in their quest to make partner or win cases, might find this to be even more true. They are expected to bill more hours, win more cases, and find time to participate in community service or political campaigns during their off-hours.

It is important that you recognize how difficult it is for your lawyer to make choices when every part of his/her professional life is demanding that it be the top priority. It is difficult for your lawyer to make the choices that you may wish him/her to make. Attention lawyers: Working 70 hours a week in the hopes of making partner in five years might mean missing your children's first years, which can never be regained. Joining an organization that requires evening meetings, running for Bar Association president, or even golfing on weekends to network for new clients takes away from family and personal time. This is extremely difficult for both lawyers and those with whom they live. Sometimes it is important to be reminded of what Chief Justice William Rehnquist meant when he said, "For some things, there is only one time in your life that they occur!"

Gently, again, very gently, remind your lawyer that family time is also a high priority. After all, your children will only have one childhood, but the Bar Association will always be there. Help your lawyer define quality of time when quantity is not possible.

Law as a Business

The marketplace has increasingly required law firms to adopt more efficient and businesslike approaches. These financially motivated practices not only cause lawyers to feel greater stress, but feed the notion that the practice of law has become a business as distinguished from a noble profession. Choices made based on financial motivation are not always the most ethical. ("Expectations, Reality, and Recommendations for Change," *The Report of the Boston Bar Association Task Force on Professional Fulfillment*, The Boston Bar Association, 1997)

And, as law becomes more and more businesslike, many lawyers are left unable to handle the business end. Most law schools do not teach business courses—they teach a course called Business Law. So many lawyers who want to open their own practice or hang out their own shingle know what is legal, but do not have the first notion of how to run an office.

Image Problem
Just a Joke

Q: Did you hear about the lawyer hurt in an accident?
A: An ambulance stopped suddenly.

Historically, being a lawyer meant one was a member of an elite society. The legal profession was held in the highest regard. Lawyers were sought out for counsel and were the most respected members of the community. Today, there is a rash of lawyer jokes, lawyer bashing at every opportunity, and a general public distrust of the entire legal profession.

"Lack of respect and confidence seems to have developed in the public's mind for the trial practice and trial practitioners of all types," the American Bar Association (ABA) and nine other lawyers' groups said in a major policy statement. They claim "tasteless advertising"— by plaintiffs' attorneys touting potential big payouts in personal injury cases—had "no doubt" contributed to declines in public esteem.

For some people, the only exposure they have to lawyers is through advertisements. Personal injury lawyers, in particular, advertise their services in ways that many people find offensive and tasteless.

Also cited were perceptions that lawyers' work had degenerated from a "noble profession" to a "mere business enterprise" motivated more by money than by public service as officers of the court. In addition, the roundtable voiced concern about a perception of lawyers' lack of civility toward one another, "win-at-any-cost" tactics and "hardball ultimatums." ("Butt of Jokes, Lawyers Fret Over Image," Reuters, September 9, 2000)

In a presentation to the Columbus Bar Association by the author, one attorney reported that dealing with obnoxious and verbally abusive opposing counsel was his biggest stress. Law school teaches you about the law, but lawyers also need lessons in dealing with life and difficult people. "We have met the enemy, and he is us," the saying goes.

Because most of us do not set foot in a courtroom very often, the media is the major vehicle that creates the image of the legal profession to the public. And, of course while we profess to know that what we see in the media is not always true, the fact is we believe much of what we see and hear without question. We rarely hear about the normal, everyday cases that lawyers try. Television, newspapers, and the Internet publicize only the sensational cases that result in colossal fees to attorneys or the miscarriage of justice when an obviously guilty person is set free. The overwhelming majority of cases where the correct settlement is reached and a lawyer receives a standard fee, or a criminal case where the guilty person is convicted and appropriately punished are not news and therefore, go unnoticed in the media.

The field of law is a popular setting for television shows, movies, and books. Again, sensationalism comes into play in order to make the storyline exciting. Often, the lawyers are the protagonists; deceitful but charming, playboys and girls who spend more time socializing, partying, and becoming involved with their colleagues than practicing law. Sometimes, the hero is a good lawyer who must fight the immoral and even violent lawyers, who usually are in the majority. Other times, the lawyers are the villains, the evil characters who are only out to suck the blood, and money, of their victims. Of course, it is fiction and the average nice, honest lawyer just would not make good entertainment. But, it all contributes to the public's perception of lawyers and the image problem.

This is not to say that all lawyers are honest, ethical, and even competent at their jobs. Many lawyers are deceitful and rightfully contribute to the image problem. There are ethics, codes, and rules in the legal profession; however, they often are not implemented. And, unfortunately, the bad apples that continue practicing without recourse spoil the whole bunch.

Maintaining Professionalism and Competence

Attending meetings, reading journals, attending conferences—there is a lack of time and money to do all that is required to keep up with the legal profession. Maintaining the CLEs (Continuing Legal Education credits) necessary to maintain the license to practice law can be a hassle. On the positive side, however, the people who are responsible for determining each state's criteria for what constitutes material worthy of CLE credit are recognizing the need to offer seminars and workshops that include the personal side of a lawyer's life. Historically, instead of these conferences assisting in lawyer stress, they contributed to it by ignoring the whole person.

The Lawyer's Appeal

After reading the list of stresses your lawyer faces, are you suddenly appreciating the things (s)he does a little more? Of course all work, inside and outside the home, can be stressful, but you must admit the list of lawyer stresses is quite extensive. Spouses of lawyers, who are sensitive and empathic to the unique stresses of the law, have a better shot at a loving and intimate relationship.

The Results of Stress on Lawyers

Depression

Depression has been called the number one problem in the legal profession *(The Bar Leader,* Leadership of the American Bar Association, March-April, 1998) And, depression often goes hand in hand with alcohol abuse, another common problem among the legal community.

The National Institute of Mental Health provides information that can help if you or your lawyer is suffering from depression. A depressive disorder is an illness that involves the body, mood, and thoughts. It affects the way a person eats and sleeps, the way one feels about oneself, and the way one thinks about things. A depressive disorder is not the same as a passing blue mood. It is not a sign of personal weakness or a condition that can be willed or wished away. People with a depressive illness cannot merely pull themselves together and get better. Without treatment, symptoms can last for weeks, months, or years. Appropriate treatment, however, can help most people who suffer from depression.

There are a variety of antidepressant medications and psychotherapies that can be used to treat depressive disorders. Some people with milder forms may do well with psychotherapy alone. People with moderate to severe depression most often benefit from antidepressants. Most do best with combined treatment: medication to gain relatively quick symptom relief, and psychotherapy to learn more effective ways to deal with life's problems. Listed below are some of the effective ways to cope.

- Set realistic goals in light of the depression and assume a reasonable amount of responsibility.

- Break large tasks into small ones, set some priorities, and do what you can as you can.

- Try to be with other people and confide in someone; it is usually better than being alone and secretive.

- Participate in activities that may make you feel better, such as going to a movie, a ball game, or participating in physical, religious, social, or other activities.

- Expect your mood to improve gradually, not immediately. Feeling better takes time.

- It is advisable to postpone important decisions until the depression has lifted. Before deciding to make a significant transition—change jobs, get married or divorced—discuss it with others who know you well and have a more objective view of your situation.

- Remember, positive thinking will replace the negative thinking that is part of the depression and will disappear as your depression responds to treatment.

- Let your family and friends help you.

No Indictment: A Case Study

Jade was a lawyer who was thought of as efficient, competent, and self-assured. In reality, she was overburdened and depressed. Jade was a perfectionist. She unknowingly developed self-imposed, unrealistic standards and tried to live up to the exaggerated expectations she thought other people had of her. She had no true self-identity and always wore a "mask" when she was in a personal relationship. She didn't allow herself to get too close to anyone in case they might see her flaws, or her true self.

During therapy, Jade realized that her unhappiness was due to her need to live up to what she believed other people thought she should be: a person who had it all together at all times. As time went on, Jade realized that making mistakes was only human, not a total disgrace. She became aware of her irrational, negative thoughts and began to change them into positive affirmations for herself. She learned to value herself, faults and all. She started using I-statements and owning her own behavior. She evaluated what she truly wanted, not what she thought others wanted her to be. She opened herself up to friendships, and eventually married a man who loved and respected her for who she was.

Health-related problems

Many lawyers often do not go to doctors when the first signs of stress-related illnesses may occur. They tend to tough it out. Also, like other people, lawyers tend to adopt harmful habits while under stress, such as not making time for exercise and not eating a healthy diet.

Alcohol Abuse

Daicoff found an increase in alcohol use between the law students' first year and their senior year. It is not uncommon for lawyers to gather together to support each other because they believe that persons who are not lawyers simply do not understand them. The knights of that elite roundtable literally come together at a round table to relax, joust, sympathize, jab, joke and lament with each other. Unfortunately, the gathering places for many lawyers are places that serve alcoholic beverages, and lawyers might bond over more than a few too many beers. Daicoff's research states that lawyers have both a "higher incidence of psychological distress and substance abuse" than other professions (see chart in Chapter 1 titled "How Lawyers Differ From The General Population"). The American Bar Association, along with many state bar associations, is addressing this issue. Substance abuse is a topic recognized worthy of CLEs and is often combined with courses in Ethics.

Divorce

It is not uncommon within the legal community to find that the stress of the profession has had a monumental effect on marriages. Many lawyers do not handle their anger well and are quick to judge and criticize. If marriages under stress do not get relief by the participants seeking professional help, which is difficult for many attorneys, divorce is the end result. If you are unhappy in your "lawyer marriage" we strongly encourage you to talk with a therapist who understands your situation and seek some help for yourself. You might need to speak with several therapists before you find the right fit. Often, the spouse may come in for help after you start the process. If nothing else, they will go in just to tell their side! Many a lawyer has come into Dr. Travis' office with the understanding (s)he was there to help a spouse, and ended up wanting help for him/herself.

Burnout

Burnout is the loss of energy and purpose resulting from stress, frustration, and boredom. Burnout is simply a depletion of energy. It can be compared to a light bulb that burns out when the energy is blocked somewhere in the system. The bulb, the wiring, the switch, or the fuse could be the problem. No matter how hard one tries to turn on the light, if the energy is depleted or blocked, the light does not turn on. The human mind works in the same way. When energy is depleted, passion, enthusiasm, and positive thoughts disappear. Burnout results in symptoms that mimic major depression, including sleep disruption, loss of appetite or binge eating, loss of motivation, listlessness, and fatigue.

A lawyer who is experiencing job burnout has their energy blocked, or has expended it without refueling. This is the cycle that promotes career dissatisfaction. The energy and zest for work becomes depleted. Lawyers in this stage begin to say, "Practicing law just isn't fun anymore." This situation occurs for a variety of reasons. Generally, people are unhappy when there is no reward for work, be it financial or personal.

Order in the Court

In counseling with couples, the power struggle over whose day has been the most difficult is often reported. Most lawyers feel as though they spend every day on a battlefield and when they come home, they really desire peace and calm. Often you feel your day has been just as stressful. After all, you have your own battlefield in the business world, corporate scene, kindergarten, or at home running the family business. Regardless, competing with your lawyer never brings satisfaction. What does work is giving sympathy and demonstrating evidence of understanding lawyer stress. Often, perhaps when you may least expect it, you receive support for your difficult times. Break the cycle today when you come together. Do not wait for magic— or your lawyer. Just do it!

Leaving the Profession

Law is increasingly reported as a profession in which its members are deeply unsatisfied. Could the reason be that the same dynamics that create a successful lawyer professionally wreak havoc in the lawyer's personal satisfaction? Lawyers are taking a closer look at their values and their sense of inner satisfaction. Some are leaving the field of law to become teachers, business people, and other professionals. A recent positive trend is for law firms to recognize this problem and allow for sabbaticals and mandated time off.

Feeling Overwhelmed and Out of Control

Lawyers are trained never to let the opposition, whether in a courtroom or at the bargaining table, see them sweat. They have to give the impression of being cool and collected at all times. Once a lawyer shows his emotions or stress, it is seen as a sign of weakness or that the lawyer is giving in. Lawyers need to be in control. You are likely to want to be in control also. It is possible for both of you to be in control of yourselves, but not each other!

How We Feel Out of Control

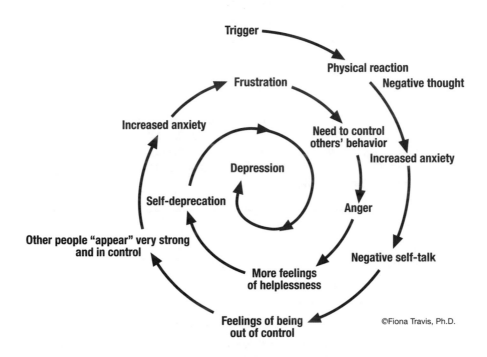

Trigger

Physical reaction

Negative thought

Frustration

Increased anxiety

Need to control others' behavior

Increased anxiety

Depression

Self-deprecation

Anger

Other people "appear" very strong and in control

Negative self-talk

More feelings of helplessness

Feelings of being out of control

©Fiona Travis, Ph.D.

The diagram on this page illustrates the phases of feeling out of control. Step one is a triggering event, which might be as simple as another person's tone of voice, look, or behavior. Steps two and three occur quickly, and practically simultaneously, on the heels of the trigger. They are a negative thought and a physical reaction. Examples of negative thoughts include "I cannot believe this" or "Here we go again." Examples of physical reactions might be a knot in the stomach, tightening of the chest, or holding the breath. Losing a sense of control is now underway.

Following the diagram, going up the left side, it indicates the other person appears to be strong and in control. The key word here is "appears." Power struggles begin at this point. In reality, that other person, perhaps the lawyer in your life, is likely feeling anxious and out of control also, and may even be feeling that *you* are the one in control.

Continuing the spiral, increased anxiety leads to attempts at controlling others' behaviors. This is a hopeless goal and is likely to lead to more intense power issues. You feel worse, helpless, self-deprecatory and end up in a state of depression. You can never control the behavior of others. You can only choose how you are going to respond.

Author's note: When suggesting that trying to control others is unhealthy, this refers to adult interactions with other adults. It certainly is a parental responsibility to control the dangerous and harmful behaviors of young infants and children.

Coping With Stress

If you do not want to spiral down this road, then don't! You are in charge of your own destiny. Stop, turn around, and go the opposite direction. Stop dead in your tracks. Notice your breathing and your negative thoughts. What are the "shoulds" going on in your head? Stop "shoulding" yourself, exhale slowly, and move into positive energy.

Do not be self-critical. When you become more aware, symptoms may become exaggerated. As a result, you may think you are actually getting worse. You are not. You are just noticing what has always been there. Think of putting your house up for sale. Wow! You think, there seem to be so many more houses up for sale than ever before. Before what? Before you were aware of them all. There are no more houses on the market than before, you are just now noticing them because that is your focus.

Maintain a sense of humor. Laugh at how difficult this process can be or how easy it is to fall into the same old patterns. For every negative belief and thought you have, there is a positive counterpart. There is no up without a down, no inside without an outside, no north without a south and no bad without a good.

It is not easy to find the positive when everything seems negative at the moment. It is more difficult to make the necessary change of direction the further along the spiral you have traveled. Therefore, awareness of the first three steps is crucial to the success of maintaining a sense of feeling in control of yourself.

Identify:

1. Your recurring triggers.

2. Your physical reaction when the trigger occurs.

3. Your negative thought at the time.

Use the spiral. Write down your triggers. How do you characteristically react? What other choices do you have?

Stress is a part of life. Examine and change the way you react to it. Awareness is the key to change. Become more aware of the problems you face and of the things you say or do that lead to problems. Next, develop methods that produce favorable results and provide some degree of relief. Finally, use these identified successful methods repeatedly in a variety of stressful situations. If you practice techniques, they will become new coping skills and will become automatically available to you when you are stressed out.

It is only after you have taken care of yourself that you can be effective helping your lawyer deal with the stress of his or her profession. This will help your relationship.

The 3 R's of Stress Reduction for Lawyers and Those Who Live with Them

Replace: Replace the negative thoughts, attitudes and behaviors that become automatic and can bog you down.

Respond: Learn and use techniques that reduce harmful effects of stress when the stress cycle gets rolling. Become aware of your breath and learn to breathe more deeply regularly throughout your day. This will help you with the "letting go" process.

Revamp: Revamp your lifestyle and reduce your stress levels. Identify your unnecessary stressors and focus on what is really important—not merely urgent—to you. Understand that in law school, lawyers are taught to react with a sense of urgency, as if there were no tomorrow. The client must be dealt with, the contract signed, the subpoena issued today. If you understand this unique dynamic of the legal profession, you can better understand your lawyer as (s)he races by.

The stress reduction techniques mentioned on the previous page are cognitive strategies. The key ingredient for calming down physically, getting grounded and centered in "sense of self" and regaining confidence is the breath. Simply the way you breathe.

A breathing technique that really works to relax your body and mind.

Find a quiet place with a smooth carpeted surface.

Lie in the Constructive Rest Position, which is on your back with your knees bent and feet flat. Do a body scan, which is simply paying attention to your body and how it is lying on the floor. Follow from the lower part of the back and slowly move your attention up the spine. Notice how much of your body is actually touching the floor. Next, focus on your breath. Just notice your breathing. What parts of your body move as you breathe?

Repeat the vowels one at a time, out loud. Say one vowel with each exhalation. Make the sound last as long as you can. Play with the sound. Hum the vowel, sing it, or just play with the sound like small children do. Have fun with each vowel. After all five vowels have been released, go back to noticing your breathing...it will be slower and much deeper. Notice how much of your body touches the floor...It will be more than before. Your muscles have relaxed and your breathing has become deeper. You are also in spinal alignment. When you have completed this process, exhale as you slowly roll to your side. Then sit up very slowly and continue to breathe slowly and deeply. Sitting up straight or too quickly just recreates all of the tension that you have just allowed to flow out of your body. You are now ready to perform any task at hand with more ease.

You can ask the lawyer in your life to join you and try the relaxation technique above, but do not be disappointed if (s)he does not want to join in. Lawyers generally as a group find nontraditional approaches out of character for them, and are uncomfortable lying on the floor making noises. A more structured, nontraditional alternative healing process may be more effective, such as Yoga, Tai Chi, or massage.

Also include in your bag of coping tricks: listening to music you like, going for a walk, talking with a close friend, gardening (digging in the dirt and weeding), taking a warm bath, reading a good book. All of the above are excellent for clearing the mind and feeding the soul.

The Sentence is... a Good Laugh

There is nothing to help you feel better than a good belly laugh. When is the last time you were able to laugh with your lawyer over something that tickled both of your funny bones? Lighten up and laugh more. Did you know laughter produces an immediate positive physical response? The breath is the key to relaxation and you cannot laugh without breathing deeply...so go for it. Love, laugh and live. There is humor everywhere. Enjoy it. "Don't take life so serious, son—it ain't no how permanent."
—Cartoonist Walt Kelly, Pogo

Did you choose to have a happy day today?

Have you reminded yourself that you are lovable?

Have you stopped a moment and enjoyed the beauty of nature?

Have you taken ten minutes to center yourself?

When did you last exhale deeply? Are you holding your breath while you are reading this page?

When did you last laugh at yourself?

When did you last give yourself a pat on the back?

Did you take pride in any small thing that you achieved today?

Are you being too self-critical?

Change your negative "tape" and play only the positive!

Getting Rid of Emotional Baggage

One lawyer shared a rule for packing when going on a trip. After packing your bags, remove half of the clothing and double the amount of money you are taking. While this might sound a bit silly, it is probably a wise thing to do in your emotional life as well. Just think: if you could remove half of the emotional baggage you carry around with you, and double your coping skills, you'd be a happier, healthier person.

Are you going through life with too much stuff packed in your carrying cases, which are your body, mind, and spirit? If you remove the unnecessary baggage, your wealth of energy will automatically double. Holding on to unnecessary thoughts and feelings will drag you down and drain your energy. So take out half of what you believe you need to hold on to, and double your wealth of energy for living your life.

Seeking Professional Help

Lawyers, male and female, have difficulty seeking help for mental or emotional health. Some believe counseling is only for the weak or crazy people in the world. The traits of the lawyer personality tend to contribute to a neglect of emotional needs. Often lawyers wait until they are desperate before seeking out professional help.

It takes a lot of courage to enter any form of therapy because it is truly a step into the unknown. You never know what you will learn about yourself or what challenges you might face. Hopefully, after reading this book, the thought of seeking help will not be so scary. Lawyers may not be psychologist-friendly, but there are psychologists who are lawyer-friendly!

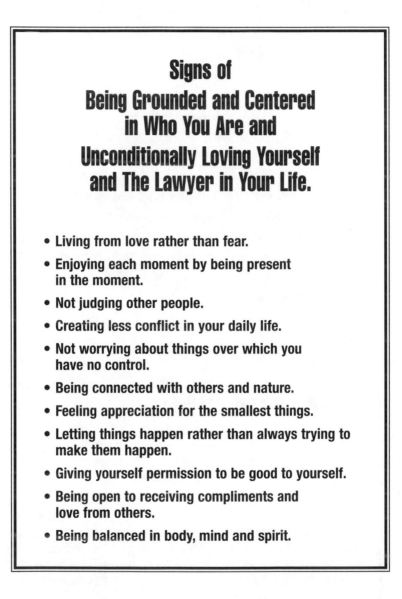

Signs of
Being Grounded and Centered in Who You Are and
Unconditionally Loving Yourself and The Lawyer in Your Life.

- Living from love rather than fear.
- Enjoying each moment by being present in the moment.
- Not judging other people.
- Creating less conflict in your daily life.
- Not worrying about things over which you have no control.
- Being connected with others and nature.
- Feeling appreciation for the smallest things.
- Letting things happen rather than always trying to make them happen.
- Giving yourself permission to be good to yourself.
- Being open to receiving compliments and love from others.
- Being balanced in body, mind and spirit.

Everyday one ought to see a fine picture, read a good poem, hear a little song, and, if it were possible, to speak a few reasonable words. —Goethe

Chapter 6

From Our
Point of View

*I disapprove of what you say,
but I will defend to the death
your right to say it.*

—Voltaire

From Our
Point of View

"Young men who feel drawn to the legal profession
may rest assured that they will find it
an opportunity for success which
is probably unequalled elsewhere."

—Louis D. Brandeis

There are various areas of the law in which an attorney can specialize. In this book, a broad concept of the general practice of law was presented. We discussed a wide spectrum of principles surrounding law school education and generalized lawyers with a lawyer-like personality based on research.

In this chapter, we give a peek into Living with our Lawyers. We include these specialties in the practice of law, because in the trial court, there are three major principals: The prosecutor or attorney for the plaintiff, the attorney for the defense, and the judge. Since we are currently living with these three roles, we chose to add a personal glimpse of them. Each of these pieces is written independently of each other and represents only each individual's personal opinion.

Living With a Judge

By Fiona Travis

"The Judge, even when he is free, is still not wholly free. He is not to innovate at pleasure. He is not a knight-errant roaming at will in pursuit of his own ideal of beauty and goodness. He is to draw his inspiration from consecrated principles."
—Benjamin Cardozo, the Nature of The Judicial Process (1921)

As discussed throughout this book, the law is an adversarial profession. Moving from a career in advocacy to the role of an impartial, objective, and fair judge can be a challenge. Judicial decisions are always subject to criticism and the general public, not always understanding how the law works, may interpret a decision they do not like or disagree with as unfair.

It is even possible that, when not happy with a judge's decision, or the manner in which a trial is proceeding, someone could become violent. This reality first struck home at my husband's swearing in ceremony. His bailiff at the time, a retired police officer, informed my mother-in-law she should not worry about her son's safety. At any sign of real trouble, he would just yell, "Hit the floor, Judge." He wanted all to know that the Judge's bench was bulletproof! I assure you, that did not make any of us feel very comfortable.

This was my first glimpse of the reality that being a judge brings with it a different kind of stress that I had not expected. For several years, I have led seminars on the transitional stress of new judges. Sponsored by the Judicial College of the Ohio Supreme Court, these seminars are designed to help newly elected or appointed judges in their transition to the bench. At each seminar, the new judges are asked what they have found most stressful about their new position. The following are some of their responses:

- The shift from a position of advocacy to one that is impartial and unbiased
- Living in the public "fish bowl"
- Emphasis on being reasonable and prudent
- Maintaining the Judicial image
- Insecurity of an elected position
- Suppressing feelings and exemplifying judicial temperament
- Making many decisions quickly, efficiently, and wisely every day
- Sense of isolation (especially from previous colleagues)
- Others' expectations of my being "all knowing" and wise
- Having to run for election, but not being political

Although none of these new judges expressed fear for his or her life, there are stressors which do threaten the ego as well as financial and job security. These same stressors can affect those of us who live with judges as well.

The American Bar Association reported the effects being married to a judge can have on the judicial spouses. Some felt their lives enhanced: "The judge works fewer hours." "There is a new status in the community." "We see new people."

Others felt deprived: "He works longer hours." "We can't entertain fellow lawyers like we once did." "She tells me to avoid politics because of the Code of Judicial Conduct." These reactions show that becoming a judge brings a variety of changes to the life of a spouse as well.

The lives of the children also change when a parent becomes a judge. One child said, "When dad was an attorney, we entertained informally. Now that he is a judge, he is a stuffed shirt, and entertainment is stiff and formal." Another reported, "My grades have improved at school since my mom became a judge, but it is not because I am a better student." ("The Family Effect," *The Judge's Book,* National Conference of State Trial Judges)

So, what is it like, living with a judge? Well, after he was first appointed to the court, my family and I addressed my husband as "Your Honor" and stood each time he entered the room. After three days, he begged us to stop!

Seriously, once he became a judge, he lost his name. Everyone now calls him Judge. "Hi Judge, how are you?" "Good to see you, Judge!" "What's new, Judge?" Even our friends who telephone ask, "How's the Judge?" or "Is the Judge there?"

For awhile, I feared that our little grandson would start calling him Grandpa Judge. However, thankfully, he is just Pop. What a relief!

Certainly, a judge deserves the respect and the honor this title brings. I am very proud when I am with him and he is referred to as "Your Honor" or "Judge." Of course, as a psychologist, I want to be sure that being renamed Judge remains an asset and does not diminish his own sense of identity. Referring to someone by his occupation identifies what he does as opposed to who he is. So, each day, whenever the opportunity arises, I remind him and others that he also a great pianist, a gourmet cook, a pretty good gardener, and an extraordinarily sensitive man (for a lawyer).

When my husband was a newly graduated lawyer, both he and I believed that judges "retired" to the bench. Only the wisest and most experienced lawyers were chosen for that honor, whether elected or appointed. Today, however, young lawyers fresh from law school plan to become judges as soon as the law permits. They are on a judicial career track with the bench as their target. As a result, many lawyers are appointed or elected to judgeships possessing only the minimum legal requirements, limited experience in the practice of law and with life in general. This was not so for my judge. He was sought out because he was wise, knowledgeable, fair, and experienced in many areas of the law. And although not aged, he is mature (most of the time)!

Being a judge is an honorable position. The responsibility is a major one and requires wisdom and integrity. Judges make life-altering decisions on a daily basis. New judges at my seminars reported that they felt pressured by having to make many decisions quickly, efficiently, and wisely every day. This can be stressful. However, for some judges, professional decisions are easier to make than personal ones.

For example, my judge will be the first to admit that although he makes significant professional decisions daily, it takes months to decide what color car to buy. Not to mention what movie to see or where to dine! I guess that is one of those lawyer attributes that work so well professionally,...and...perhaps, not so well personally. Although this can drive me a bit crazy when it is car buying time, I confess that I am truly proud of the thoughtfulness, compassion, and yes, sometimes the agony, that goes into the process of being sure he is making the right decision.

Federal judges are appointed for life. However, many state judges are either elected or must face a retention election process after an initial appointment. In those states where they are elected by the voting public, judges are considered non-partisan. Most, however, are endorsed by one of the two major political parties. As a result, politics can be involved in the process.

Normally, judicial races differ from the campaigns of other elected officials. The Cannons of Judicial Ethics are very strict and are designed to make sure that judges remain unbiased and objective. These ethical standards prohibit judicial candidates from speaking on any issues which may come before the court. As a result, judicial races generally do not draw much public attention and some consider them very boring.

Many who pride themselves on voting fail to vote in judicial races. Perhaps it is because the races are not particularly exciting. It may be that many believe their lives will not be affected by the legal system, or it may be that many perceive judges to be aloof, far removed, and not connected to the general public. Regardless of the reason, it remains a fact that judicial races receive less attention than those of other elected positions, while still requiring a lot of time, energy and money to run a campaign.

The courts can be intimidating and many people are not really clear on what judges do. Yes, today there is Court TV where one is exposed to actual courtroom proceedings. However, people continue to misunderstand the judicial process, especially when a decision or an opinion of the judge is not what they think it should be. Criticism of the court often results. Most do not understand that what might appear to them as "fair" or unfair" may not have anything to do with the law by which a judge must rule.

Hopefully, people will become more aware of the significant role our judiciary plays in history. As I was writing this passage, our nation was waiting to learn the results of the presidential election of 2000, reportedly the closest presidential race in 124 years. The decision ultimately ended up in the hands of, guess who? Yes, the Justices of The Supreme Court of the United States. The eyes of the nation were upon these nine men and women as everyone waited to learn how they would interpret the Constitution and how their decision would impact who our next president would be.

Whether you agree with the result or not, a sharply divided court was able to reach a decision, which will be closely examined by legal scholars for years to come. This book is not about that process, nor the legal issues involved. Rather, the controversial decision exemplifies how decision making can bring about extraordinary stress for a judge.

All judges, not just Supreme Court Justices, are subjected to controversy surrounding their decisions. In Chapter 5, one of the stressors identified was the professional image of the legal profession. Lawyers and judges are concerned with this problem.

Dissenting from the result in the U.S. Supreme Court decision which so dramatically affected the presidential election, Mr. Justice John Paul Stevens wrote: "Although we may never know with complete certainty, the identity of the winner of this year's presidential election, the identity of the loser is perfectly clear; it is the nation's confidence in the Judge as an impartial guardian of the law."

Regardless of one's political point of view, Justice Steven's words should be cause for concern in all of us. Hopefully, in the future, voters will pay more attention to those "boring" judicial races; and to the races of those elected officials who will be appointing our judiciary. Although imperfect and highly criticized, our legal system is still the best in the world and protects our democracy.

So, what is like, living with a judge? It is my honor, Your Honor.

Living With a Criminal Defense Attorney

By Frances Weiner

"In Germany, they came first for the communists, and I did not speak up because I wasn't a communist. They came for the Jews, and I didn't speak up because I wasn't a Jew.

Then they came for the trade unionist, and I didn't speak up because I wasn't a trade unionist. Then they came for the Catholics, and I didn't speak up because I was protestant.

Then they came for me, and by that time, no one was left to speak up."

—Martin Neimoller, German prisoner of war and protestant minister

I am proud to be married to Sam Weiner for 23 years. He was 34 and I was 30 when we were married. Obviously, by that time in our lives, we each had developed well defined values, morals, and beliefs. He had already been a prosecutor and at that time was working for a small law firm, specializing in criminal defense work. A short time after our courtship began, I learned his dream was to open his own law practice.

He convinced me to marry him when he said, "I believe you can help me become the best that I can be." No one had ever bestowed such trust and honor in me, and as a result, I found my partner in life.

Before we were married, I had convinced him to buy a small building, and shortly thereafter, he opened his own criminal defense practice. Although a sole practitioner, since he had involved me in every aspect of creating the physical environment of his office, I felt as though the practice was "ours" together and not just his alone.

My initial involvement was limited to being a "sounding board." I was a lay person who could represent opinions as a member of a jury. In the evenings as we took long walks, he would share facts and I would relate how I was affected by his proposed defense.

We are from very different backgrounds with very different histories; add to that gender differences and obviously, we did not always agree. I believe that my husband's clients have benefited from our collaborative efforts.

My lifelong fascination with the human mind seduced me into getting emotionally involved in my husband's cases. I was a naive, young woman with a gigantic heart and believed my husband's clients simply never learned "right from wrong."

Occasionally, when my husband felt a client was serious about making positive changes in life, he would suggest that they call and talk with me. Many have called over the years. Most, unfortunately, have not been able to work as hard as one needs to work in order to make a lifestyle change. It is not easy to reach teens and adults who do not realize that earning an honest minimal wage is better than lots of money from selling cocaine. Although my guidance, coaching and counseling has not made a major impact, there is nothing more satisfying than hearing one of his clients say, "Thank you for helping me change my life." Although I do not charge for my personal coaching, I do request a donation to a charitable organization that they choose. I learned a long time ago the free advice is never heeded.

As a lay person who represented the jury, I knew if I didn't get it, neither would they. Ralph D. Emerson once wrote: "Eloquence is the power to translate a truth into language perfectly intelligible to the person to whom you speak." I was a tough juror. My husband was forced to use analogies, metaphors and visuals to get his point across. At this point, I must confess that I am multilingual with English being my fifth language. I learned it at the age of 15 when I came to this country. So you see, I had a perfect excuse to make my husband constantly search for better ways to effectively clarify and tie together complex facts and legal concepts.

I was not just being "mean." It was my bleeding heart that led my husband to use expert psychologists 20 years ago. They were rarely used at that time. Surely only an insane person could kill another and only someone totally deprived of love and proper socialization could rape, rob and steal. Consequently, most of my husband's clients had to be psychologically evaluated. My husband was among the first attorneys in Ohio to use the "Battered Woman Syndrome" as a defense in homicide cases and he even employed Lenore Walker, Ph.D., innovator of the concept.

The Supreme Court of the State of Ohio requires that each lawyer receive 12 hours of continuing legal education every year in order to maintain a license to practice law in our state. My husband often lectures at these seminars, as well as attends conferences in other states. I accompany him in nearly every instance and our personal relationship developed over time to where other lawyers' wives sought out my advice on how to better relate with, and assist, their husbands. I have also had the privilege of personally meeting great criminal defense attorneys, among them Bobby Lee Cook, Albert Kreiger, Gary Spence, and Richard (Racehorse) Haines.

As time went on, I became more and more aware that the specialty of criminal defense was socially misunderstood. In order for me to better understand why this was happening and how lawyers were contributing to it, I suggested that my husband get involved in professionally related organizations. I believe that mingling with one's peers is an invaluable experience. He followed my advice and to date, his achievements in professional organizations are matched by few, if any, in the state of Ohio. He holds many honors.

As a result of the social aspects of these many organizations, I have had the opportunity to meet many more lawyers' wives and each has disclosed to me the difficulty encountered in social settings as a result of living with a criminal defense attorney. Interestingly enough, it is the spouses of the lawyers who receive the negative comments. As a result of these experiences, I decided to become more involved and more educated so that I could become a relentless defender and spokesperson for the practice of criminal defense law!

As a career wife, I believe that I have a unique function to serve—to educate the public about the importance of the role that criminal defense attorneys play in our society. The criminal defense attorney:

- Assures adherence to the presumption of innocence
- Insists the government's burden of proof be met in seeking a conviction
- Fosters respect for the system of trial by jury
- Improves the public understanding of constitutional guarantees that protect us all, not only persons accused of crimes
- Takes a leading role in upholding constitutional rights

By doing all of these, I believe they are relentless Champions of Liberty.

Living with one of these Champions of Liberty, however, has its price. As the streets get meaner and the government gets more anxious to prosecute, the police are forced, on some occasions, to overreact and fabricate. I believe my husband, by doing his job during cross-examination, might become vulnerable to a policeman or informant who does not understand it is not a personal issue. Nor would they understand that they need to remain professional, and not to take his cross-examination personally.

In my 23 years, we never feared a client. No client ever asked my husband to do something unethical. They have all understood that he is bound by ethical considerations and have respected him for it. As a rule, we never socialize with clients. It is our belief that it is hard to remain objective and professional when doing so, and there is a risk of inadequate representation of the client in favor of socializing.

Another negative of our life together is the need to be careful with whom we associate. This is done in order not to expose ourselves to misunderstandings that, although baseless, could become problems. In some social circles, people are afraid to be seen with a criminal defense attorney, for fear of being mistaken as one of our clients. The truth is, all professions have their negatives and positives, but other professions do not seem to have as broad a social impact as do criminal defense lawyers. It's not easy being a defender of liberty.

In the hopes of helping someone who may be involved with a criminal defense attorney, let me share some commonly asked questions which come up to the significant others in such a relationship. The answers to these questions are born of my 23 years of experience as a career wife.

Q. "How can he defend those people?"

"Who are those people?" "Those people" are human beings with frailties of human nature and of the demonic forces which sometimes can drive the best of us to some form of self-destruction. They come from all walks of life. They live in all neighborhoods. In today's world a client might be a social equal, a neighbor, a former schoolmate, children of colleagues or from an organization of which the lawyer is a member. They are of all races, creeds and religions. Personally, I do not think it is an issue of "who" my husband defends as much as it is a question of "what" he is defending. And that "what" is liberty and justice for all.

**Q.	"Oh, so your husband is a criminal attorney?"**

Now, that makes me wince. No, there is nothing
criminal about him! If there were, he would not be
permitted to practice law. The reality is my husband
represents the accused. And many of his clients are
found "not guilty." He is a lawyer working in the
criminal justice system.

**Q.	"How could he get that guy off?"**

This question demonstrates a plethora of misconcep-
tions and misinformation people have about the legal
system. The attorney's responsibility is to represent his
client to the best of his ability, to challenge the state's
evidence, to sensitize the jury to the skepticism necessary to support reasonable doubt and to generate compassion for the client. It is the jury who must determine
whether or not the prosecution has met its burden of
proof beyond a reasonable doubt.

Should the jury conclude that the state has failed to meet that
burden, then it is their sworn duty to find the accused not guilty.
So you see, therefore, it is not an issue of "getting someone off."
It is a failure of proof.

When I married, I still naively believed that civilization had
evolved and would continue to evolve, and that by twists and turns,
our society would someway or another, become more civil and
compassionate and cultured, with liberty and justice for all. As my
awareness grew, I was rudely awakened by the reality of politics
and the dangerous role it plays in the law. The nation has lost its
collective soul when crime became the number one political issue
for both Democrats and Republicans. The same people who have
been preaching less government now demand more police, more
prosecutors and more prisons. Instead of spending money on

attacking the root cause of crime by providing housing, education, training and rehabilitation, our politicians are promising to increase imprisonment and state sanctioned executions.

The American family is at its nadir. With media glorifying violence, both parents working, and high divorce rates, the children's needs are not met. We are now seeing the tragic effect this has on children involved in the school shootings in Colorado and Georgia.

I disagree with the White House slogan "It takes a village." I believe in personal responsibility and accountability, not more government. The current system of mandatory sentencing needs to be revisited; it limits the range of a judge's discretion and limits the range of advocacy for the lawyer. I believe the passions aroused by the human cry for vengeance can give way to calm. I like to believe that the evolution of our species has not ended. Pascal (17th century philosopher and scientist) said,

"We arrive at the truth, not by reason only but by heart."

My husband has dedicated his life and has put his heart and soul into the representation of the criminally accused. There are many sleepless nights. Pressure and stress are part of his everyday existence. A case lost can mean his client's freedom or, worse yet, his life. He is a man who loves justice and believes in individual freedom. He has integrity and courage, which one must have in order to withstand the dysfunction introduced by a criminal defense practice.

The following are the qualities and skills my husband takes into the courtroom every day: intelligence, creativity, knowledge of the law, common sense, compassion, his great ability to persuade and convince others. He has foresight and anticipation, he is prepared and organized, he is in charge, he is sincere, he uses good judgment and regardless of circumstances, he keeps his composure. He has the role of being a psychological support to his client and his client's family while undergoing the horrors of prosecution. He understands the responsibility that each one of the cases carries. He is fighting to retain our precious rights and liberties as American citizens as well of those of the accused, one case at a time.

The journey I began 23 years ago by marrying a criminal defense attorney has helped define who I am. It has not only increased my self-growth and awareness, but it has also increased my social awareness, and added purpose to my life. I believe that who we are is the sum total of our experiences and that, as long as we live, we experience and learn, therefore, we grow. I feel a great deal of who I have become is directly linked to the experiences afforded me by living with a criminal defense attorney. The gains have been immeasurable.

As citizens, we are affected by a variety of issues at the local, state, and national levels. Some of us attempt to meet these challenges, and make a difference by helping those in need; we do this by diligently voting and by making financial contributions to support causes of concern to us. Many, however, resist taking any kind of responsibility. They find it easier, instead, to look to others to solve all of the world's problems. Rather than take any active role in gaining and maintaining certain rights, they feel no responsibility for making clear choices about the quality of their citizenship. Eldridge Cleaver, during the 1960s, wrote,

"If you are not part of the solution, then you are part of the problem."

Not everyone can have the impact of a Rosa Parks, but we can each take a stand in the struggle against injustice. William Faulkner once wrote in a speech,

"Never be afraid to raise your voice for honesty and truth and compassion against injustice and lying and greed. If people all over the world, in thousands of rooms like this one, would do this, it would change the earth."

There is only one Constitution, and it protects all of us or none of us. It is up to all of us to take an active role to protect the Constitution and the Bill of Rights. We live in a high-technology world, where the Government can monitor our cellphones, track our e-mail, and determine our whereabouts through our computers. We are all at risk of losing our privacy. All of us should start paying attention.

I believe that understanding all this; those living with criminal defense attorneys have the awesome responsibility of supporting and loving them. We are what is decent in their world. We are their balance. At the end of the day, those of us living with a criminal defense attorney get whatever was not left in the courtroom. In order to live successfully with the criminal defense lawyer in your life, I offer my personal suggestions:

- Have your own sense of self
- Be mature
- Be interdependent as opposed to dependent
- Be flexible
- Have compassion
- Ask not what he or she can give to you, but rather ask what you can give to him or her

Remember, you can't change anyone, but you can change yourself. I hope my part of this chapter will provide profound new insights to guide you in your continuing journey of self-discovery and successful living with the criminal defense attorney in your life. Take good care of yourself and the lawyer in your life. If you want to fax me, please do so at (614) 443-9978. I can't promise you I'll have the answer or great insight, but I will try. In the end that's all any of us can do.

Living With a Prosecuting Attorney

By Julia DeVillers

"Men are not hanged for stealing horses, but that horses may not be stolen."
—*First Marquis of Halifax*

The goal of a prosecutor is not to convict people, but to end crime. Convictions are merely a means to that end. Convictions, even of the clearly guilty, must be accomplished within the parameters of the Constitution. Contrary to common belief, the prosecutor's job is not simply to put the accused in jail. It is to preserve justice. Thus, if a prosecutor has significant doubts of the guilt of a defendant, he has a responsibility to dismiss the case. And, even if a prosecutor is convinced of the guilt of a defendant, if the evidence against the accused was collected in a manner contrary to the Constitution, he has a duty to disclose such a violation.

Prosecutors:

- Enforce laws by prosecuting violators
- Represent a city or county in civil matters
- Research and argue pretrial motions
- Litigate cases
- Write briefs and argue appeals
- Assist and advise police in criminal investigations
- Negotiate pleas with defense attorneys
- Interview lay and expert witnesses
- Advise victims of their rights

As the wife of an assistant prosecutor, I take pride in what my husband does for a living. When people ask what he does for a living and I answer "He's a prosecutor," they often respond, "Oh, he's one of the good guys." The perception is that prosecutors are the heroes of the justice system, fighting crime and keeping we, the people, safe. Personally, I believe that perception is absolutely true. I do think that prosecution is a noble profession. It is gratifying to witness violent criminals—rapists, murderers, thieves, child abusers—being taken off the streets and locked away, knowing that my husband has had played a major role in that process.

My husband has an excellent awareness of the power and responsibility of a prosecutor. I remember asking my husband when he first took this job if he was concerned that he would convict an innocent person. Then he taught me how the system works. I was under the impression the prosecutor's job is to convict the people in their cases, regardless of what they believed. However, a prosecutor only has to prosecute people if (s)he is convinced of their guilt. On the other hand, a defense attorney who is convinced of the guilt of his client has an ethical obligation to defend him regardless of what he believes. My husband has had cases, including murder cases, that he has dismissed because he was not convinced that a person is guilty. On every occasion, his office has backed his decision. Of course, the system is not perfect and my husband strongly supports the use of DNA and other methods that may free the truly innocent.

Due to the laws of this state, my husband argues for the death penalty in some cases. While I personally am still trying to solidify my views on the issue of capital punishment, I recognize that there are persuasive arguments in its favor. Deterrence and retribution are the common ends my husband and his colleagues truly believe derive from capital punishment. These are the intellectual arguments for the death penalty. But I find that the people asking the above question are usually not asking how my husband can handle such cases on an intellectual level but rather on an emotional one.

The answer is that it is often easier on an emotional level. One has to remember that the prosecutor spends his or her time with the victims of these cases. He feels the pain, anger and sorrow of the victim's family and even the victim. The prosecutor goes to the crime scene, sees the autopsy photos, talks to the witnesses. He knows every little detail of the victim's last moments of life. He is presently trying a capital case where a 14-year-old girl and her boyfriend were abducted, taken to a cornfield and executed. They were killed because the boyfriend was a witness to a murder. The murder had been committed by the defendant's fellow gang member. The innocent girl just happened to be in the wrong place at the wrong time. Feeling sorry for the defendant is difficult in cases such as these.

Being a prosecutor is a demanding and stressful job. Some trials can last weeks. Many prosecutors have a difficult time focusing on their home lives during trials. They are often thinking about the next day's arguments. When the average person sees a trial it is immediately evident that the consequences to the defendant are great. If he is convicted he will be imprisoned or even executed. However, far worse to the public is the consequence of a guilty person going free and back to the streets. Besides the potential threat to the general public, there can be a threat to the witnesses. A great deal of my husband's time is spent convincing witnesses to testify. Witnesses, especially to violent crimes, know that if the defendant is acquitted they may be the next victim. My husband also knows this, and the pressure is on to keep everybody safe.

People ask me if my husband despises all criminal defense attorneys. I myself can't help but occasionally question how a person could try to set a defendant free when they know that the defendant is guilty, particularly those who have committed a violent crime. Yet I recognize their role in society is necessary. Every prosecutor I have talked to considers criminal defense attorneys colleagues, not enemies. They don't have a case "against" defense attorney Sam Weiner, they have a case "with" Sam Weiner. Most cases end in negotiated plea bargains. As such, cordial relationships are necessary. When in trial, however, they are in "battle." They argue to the judge, they argue to the jury, they argue with each other. At times these arguments are very heated. But an hour after closing arguments, they go have a drink with each other. Respect breeds friendship. Some of our closest friends are criminal defense attorneys. Many of whom are ex-prosecutors who, as my husband says, "were seduced by the dark side."

Prosecutors spend more time in the courtroom than most other attorneys, which is where the excitement is. Being a prosecutor can be high profile and even glamorous. But on the downside, prosecutors work for the government. Government salaries are generally low, and to be an assistant prosecutor means you are likely going to struggle with those law school loans for awhile. The caseload is high and long drawn out trials can mean eighteen-hour workdays. However, most of the prosecutors I know love what they do. You won't get rich being a prosecutor.

And, while the public often considers the prosecutor the "good guy," the criminals certainly don't. My husband is the director of the gang unit for our county, and has been the subject of several death threats and there is word of a contract on his life. Thus, while violence toward a prosecutor is extremely rare, we still have to be cautious. As I write this book, I have two SWAT police officers with a car full of weapons I don't wish to see, sitting on my street guarding our house. They accompany me and my family members wherever I go. When my husband took the job, I wasn't anticipating bodyguards. Or receiving a phone call that I have to suddenly take my family out of town until "things blow over" and the threats on my husband's life subside. However, the disadvantages are outweighed by the rewards of knowing that the men, women, and children in my community are safer because of what my husband is doing.

Conclusion

We have shared some glimpses into the relationship with the lawyer in our lives, and we sincerely hope that you have learned some ways to take care of yourself with the lawyer in your life. As a parting gift to you, we have condensed some healthy strategies that you might be able to recall when needed by simply spelling out the word LAWYERS.

7 Keys to Successful Living With Lawyers

L = Learn, Listen, and Lighten up.

Learn: You have learned ways to successfully live with your lawyer by reading this book. Use what you have learned in your daily interactions. Remember the Lawyer Personality. Practice the ways to keep your sense of self while maintaining a healthy relationship. Use communication skills to strengthen your relationship. And, practice stress reduction techniques with your lawyer so you can relax and enjoy your relationship and your life. Listen: The chapter on communication skills taught you about the role of the "listener." Truly listen to your lawyer when (s)he communicates something to you. Practice this skill on a daily basis. Remember, lawyers love to talk and they appreciate being heard. Lighten up: Being able to laugh lightens the burden of life. Laugh at yourself and with your lawyer.

A = Awareness.

Awareness is the key to all change. Awareness enables a response instead of a reaction. When you and your lawyer disagree, pay attention to your breath. Pay attention to your gut feelings and what they are telling you. Do not let that lawyer personality intimidate you. Remember, your lawyer has anxiety also!

W = Wholeness.

The best relationships are those in which both parties do not need each other to feel whole, but rather two whole, self-fulfilled persons who want to share their lives together. It is important in any relationship to have a sense of self outside of the other person. In order to be whole, you must have balance in your life. Know all of the roles you play, and find balance between the mental, emotional, physical, and spiritual.

Y= Yield.

Yielding does not mean being passive or giving up. In work-shops with lawyer spouses, participants practice four basic developmental movements: Yielding, Reaching, Pushing, and Pulling. These are essential movements in order for infants to get from lying in the crib to standing on their own feet. Little ones reach out, push their heads up with their hands, and eventually pull themselves up to stand. Reaching, pushing and pulling are easy to see and understand because they are active. You might think of yielding as a passive giving in and feel you will lose control if you yield.

However, the author's definition of yield is to "actively meet." Think of the yield sign on the highway. The same yield sign is on the highway of life with your lawyer—you must be able to move in the same direction and yield when necessary in order to not get run over by those strong lawyer personality attributes. Practice yielding and get on the road that leads to a compassionate relationship with your lawyer.

E = Equalize and Enjoy.

It is not easy to hold your own identity when living with a lawyer. The lawyer personality is a dominant one. By understanding that fact, you can maintain your own identity in the relationship. Opposites can complement each other. Know that you and your lawyer are different, but equal.

One of the first self-help books to hit the market was titled I'm *Ok, You're Ok: A Practical Guide to Transactional Analysis,* Re-released by Galahad Books, 1999). Just keep repeating that title over and over again when your lawyer creates any doubt which remember, they are trained to do. I'm O.K., You're O.K. It is a healthy place to be.

Enjoy. Find joy in the moment. There is a saying, "The past is history, the future is mystery, but the moment right now is a gift; that is why it is called the present."

Do not fly into the future—learn to be in the here and now. Do not postpone joy! All of life can be enjoyed. Help your lawyer do the same.

R = Relax!

Although this might be easier said than done, practicing relaxation on a daily basis is not all that difficult. Chapter 5 gave you some ideas. Find what works for you and put it into your life every day. Having gained understanding and insight into the uniqueness of lawyer stress, acceptance of yourself and your lawyer will come more readily. Help your lawyer relax. Knowing lawyer resistance, find something that is acceptable to both and do it together.

S = Self.

Take responsibility for yourself. Do not try to change your lawyer. That is an impossible task that results in feelings of frustration that ultimately lead to depression. You have choices about your daily life. Take charge of you. Make choices and return the sense of control to yourself. Pamper yourself. Find an activity that is just yours. The self is made up of all the parts of you. Do not neglect any one of them.

It is only when you are your whole self and are grounded and centered in your sense of self that you are able to truly give love to others, including the lawyer in your life. Be true to your self.

Understanding

Kindness

Consideration

Acknowledgment

Patience

Thoughtfulness

Trust

Faith

Loyalty

Charity

Hope

Additional Acknowledgments

From Fiona

The seed for this book was planted in March of 1996, while my husband and I attended a medical staff retreat through Mount Carmel Medical Center. Dr. Stan Sateren, director of medical education for Mount Carmel East, was responsible for the program and had sought out a seminar by Dr. Michael F. Myers, a psychiatrist from Vancouver, British Columbia, Canada. He is the author of *Doctors' Marriages: A Look at the Problems and Their Solutions.* He presented a three-hour workshop for the doctors and their spouses.

My thanks to Dr. Sateren for that program and Dr. Michael F. Myers whose book and seminar have continued to be an inspiration to me throughout the writing of this book.

On our way home from that medical staff retreat, my husband and I spoke about my doing a similar type of seminar for the legal profession. In order to do so, I needed to write a book. My husband was excited about this concept and readily shared his ideas. I wrote as he drove and by the time we arrived home, the book had a beginning. The seed was planted and nurtured by his encouragement; a book had already begun to take form.

There have been many people to thank who have provided the nurturing, sunshine, and the necessary "rain" of ideas to help grow the flowering concept into the book, *Living With Lawyers.* So please bear with us through the next few paragraphs as we thank the many people who spread those nutrients along the way.

Special thanks to:

My family members: Anita and Heather, my daughters-in-law, for sharing their artistic insight and talents. My brother Donald, who loves and supports me unconditionally, no matter what. My sister-in-law Lynn for always being there when I need her. My sons Todd and Craig: Todd for the ability to see humor in life, even in the most difficult of times and who exemplifies his late Grandmother Travis's favorite saying "Sweet are the uses of adversity, which like a venomous toad, yet wears a crown of jewels in its head," and to Dr. Craig, thank you for so generously sharing your knowledge gained while writing your own book and providing me with a Daily Dose of Positivity.

My family of my private practice at Columbus Psychological Center: Mary Beth Schirtzinger for sharing her wisdom about personality theory; her husband David, for saving the book when my computer crashed.

Scottie Melody for her loyalty and hard work that keeps my practice going so that I can afford to take the necessary time to write; her husband Scott, for keeping the office computer up to date and helping me get over my original computer phobia. To Tracy Morgan, Melinda Cooksey, and Liz Clark for believing in me and my work. To S.R. Thorward and Jim Althof for sharing my office so that I can cut back my clinical hours and write instead!

Sy Kleinman, my longtime, dear friend, mentor, and colleague at The Ohio State University who has managed to keep me connected to academia in a meaningful way.

Lawrence Richard of Altman Weil Legal Consultants for his ground-breaking research in the field of study about the lawyer personality, and Susan Daicoff, professor at Florida Coastal Law School for her compilation of the data and research on this subject.

A special thanks to my co-authors:

Frances, for her support, reminding me that I have unique expertise, and gently prodding me along the way from shortly after the seed was planted; and Julie, without whose knowledge, skills and expertise about the publishing business, this book would never have been completed.

From Frances

My humble and heartfelt thanks to Linda Myers for typing my work, her cheerful support, and her infectious optimism.

Special thanks to: Mike Schakett, Roco Contini, David Voyles, Barbara Jean Schaeffer, Sandy Edelberg, Lara Brown and Sherran Blair for their friendship, support and for always responding to my needs.

To the Menninger Institute, whose educational endeavors, research and work in the field of mental health have been major inspirations in my life.

To Alex LaGouch and the staff of the Columbus Bar Association for contributions to research questions asked.

From Julie

Thanks to Mary Geer for her design and extra effort, and Johannah Haney and Debra Pack for their top-notch editorial assistance.

And to Robin Rozines, Jennifer Roy, Amy Rozines, Rene and Carol DeVillers, Lori Rossi, Dawn DeVillers, Molly DeVillers, and Dawn Nocera.

INDEX

The authors are available to speak, consult, and lead workshops and seminars. They also welcome your comments and questions.

To order books or tapes
Single copies: $19.95, includes shipping and handling

Phone toll-free 1-866-LIVELAW
E-mail: sales@livingwithlawyers.com
or contact Quarry Publishing
6468 Quarry Lane
Dublin, Ohio 43017

To reach:
Dr. Fiona Travis: drtravis@livingwithlawyers.com
or contact Columbus Psychological Center
4700 Reed Road, Suite A
Columbus, OH 43220
614-457-0024
FAX: 614-457-0026
Frances Weiner: Fax: 614-443-9978
Julia DeVillers: Julia@livingwithlawyers.com

Relaxation tapes titled "Letting Go...An Integrated Approach to Relaxation" by Drs. Craig and Fiona Travis are available and complement the content of this book. Set of two 90-minute audiotapes are available for $19.95 per set. Please ask us about our combined book and tape package rate.

Please visit our website for further information
www.livingwithlawyers.com